Peter Harriso
PC Crash Course Series

PC CRASH COURSE &
SURVIVAL GUIDE

Thank you for buying this product from **PC Productions Limited**, and welcome to our fast growing user-group. We hope that you will be fully satisfied with this course, and also enjoy using it.

PC Productions Limited does not provide any guarantees whatsoever regarding the contents of this course and reserves the right to make improvements and/or changes in the course, or any accompanying materials, whenever necessary or advisable. Any error in content or typography will be corrected in the next edition.

System requirements:

In order to use this product fully you need the following:

⊕ An IBM™ or compatible PC.

Exercise diskette

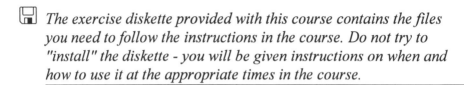 *The exercise diskette provided with this course contains the files you need to follow the instructions in the course. Do not try to "install" the diskette - you will be given instructions on when and how to use it at the appropriate times in the course.*

Published by:
PC Productions Limited
The Clock House
Stafford Mill
STROUD
GL5 2AZ
U.K.

Tel: 01453-755200
Fax: 01453-755400

ISBN 1 873005 14-8

Your exercise diskette

 The diskette that accompanies this course contains the files you will need to follow the exercises in the course. <u>You will find instructions on how to use your diskette as you progress through the manual</u>.

There is no need to install the diskette on your computer.

Conventions used in the course

To make it easier to understand and use this course we have used different typefaces as explained below.

Instructions

Instructions are preceded by a dot, e.g.:

• Make sure your printer is switched on and ready to go.

Items that you are to type on the keyboard are printed in a different typeface and indented, e.g.:

• Type:

   Type this now!

Whenever specific keys, buttons or options are referred to, we print the item in bold type, as follows:

• Press the **Enter** key,

or,

• Click **OK**.

Key combinations

Key combinations are sometimes referred to with a plus sign between two keys. This means that the two keys should be pressed together, e.g.:

• Press **Shift+F8**

If two keys are separated by a comma then the keys should be pressed one after the other, e.g.:

• Press **Home, ArrowDown**.

General points

Items making a general point, which are not instructions to carry out immediately, are shown as follows:

☻ You could also have used the **Print Preview** feature.

Screen text

Items that refer to something displayed on your screen are shown underlined or in a separate frame, e.g.

This is text that appears on your screen.

or,

```
This is displayed on your screen
```

Notes

Notes providing information to be remembered are shown as follows:

 If you make a mistake typing in text or commands, you can press the **Backspace** *key to delete the letter you just typed.*

Notes about learning

 It is a very good idea to make your own notes as you progress. Actually going through the process of making notes and summarizing your thoughts will help you to remember.

Always try to complete the chapter you are working with rather than breaking off in the middle.

There is no doubt that experimentation will help you learn. At the end of each chapter, feel free to experiment on your own. The further through the course you get, the more confidence you will gain. That's when you should start experimenting.

Quick Contents

Before you start

The sheer volume of things to be learnt when you start off in computers can be rather daunting to say the least. It is not the intention of this book to replace any of the original documentation you may have acquired - in a book of this size and scope it would be impossible. However, it is our intention, using language that is easy to understand and examples that are easy to follow, to guide you through the most important features of exactly what a PC is, and how you use one. It is our aim to assist you in gaining the basic knowledge you will require to do all the common tasks that more experienced users seem to do with ease, such as copying and deleting files, formatting diskettes and organising your hard disk.

The structure of this course

This course has 24 chapters and 3 appendices which can be divided into 4 main sections as follows:

Chapters	*Description*
1 - 7	General introduction and information about PC's, hardware and software.
8-16	A solid practical guide to the basics of DOS, teaching you to format diskettes, copy and delete files and to create and work with subdirectories.
17 - 24	These chapters are a little more advanced and will take you one step further on. They cover, amongst other things, backing up files, undelete, memory, defragmenting disks and viruses.
Appendices A-D	A general introduction to Windows, a summary of the most common DOS commands and error messages and an introduction to batch files.

Table of Contents

Contents

Contents

PC - What's That?

The initials PC stand for *Personal Computer*, the collective name given to a whole range of computers found at work and in the home. This chapter will give you a little background history and a brief introduction to personal computers.

A little history

The first electronic computer was produced as long ago as 1946. It was called ENIAC, and comprised more than 18,000 vacuum tubes, the kind used in old-fashioned radio and television sets. As you can imagine it was a very large machine, occupying most of a whole building. It weighed 30 tons, which is about as much as 30 small cars. ENIAC was in use for about 10 years, but despite its colossal size it could not do more than a simple pocket calculator can do today.

ENIAC and an early PC.

In 1975, the first home computers were launched. Amongst the first producers were such familiar companies as Apple, Commodore, and Tandy. Atari launched its first computer aimed at both home users and small companies in 1979, and about a year later the first small business computers, such as the Osborne I and Kaypro II, were launched.

A very significant year for the development of computers was 1981, when IBM launched its first personal computer. Since then, computers have developed amazingly quickly. Today's personal computers are faster, have a much larger capacity, and cost only a fraction of a 1981 model.

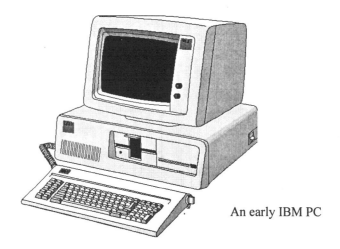

An early IBM PC

Many companies adopted the standards set by the IBM PC to produce their own computers, which work in the same way as the IBM machines. These are often referred to as *IBM compatible* computers, or IBM clones. Both the IBM PC and compatible PCs have undergone enormous development, with improvements being announced every few months. This has resulted in newer models with names such as the XT, AT, 286, 386, 486, Pentium and PS/2. These different models are discussed in more detail in the next chapter.

What is a computer really?

In simple terms, a computer is no more than an electrical appliance. Like your television, or freezer, it has been developed to be able to perform certain tasks. For example, you can use your computer as a typewriter for writing letters, or as a pocket calculator to do your sums. You can also use it to store telephone numbers, play games, produce technical drawings and develop camera-ready documents for printing. Computers can even be used to run production lines. Just like any other electrical appliance, computers can and do break down and cause problems. However, be very sceptical when a mistake is blamed "on the computer". In most cases it's a human error that causes you to receive that notice from the 'phone company that says that unless you pay your outstanding bill for £4,567,333, your telephone will be disconnected.

A computer is not some sort of supernatural, super-intelligent, all-mighty machine, poised to take over the world. A computer can not think for itself, it can only follow instructions. It is not capable of suddenly deciding that it would like to have an ice-cream cone, or of feeling the desire to take a long vacation on some sunny island beach.

A computer can however, follow instructions and perform pre-defined tasks at an amazingly high rate: a million or so instructions per second.

Assume that you have a list of telephone numbers stored in your computer system, and a program, or pre-defined list of instructions, which can extract the right number for a given person. If you ask your computer what telephone number Abraham Lincoln has, it will probably, after a short delay, tell you that it can not find his number. It is not capable, however, of answering directly that Lincoln was alive 200 years ago and does not, and did not, have a telephone.

If you ask your computer to print out "2+5=9", it will do so. Again it is not capable of thinking for itself and telling you that 2+5 does not equal 9. It can't refuse to print lies. On the other hand, by giving the computer the right information it could, for example, calculate the wages for thousands of employees in a large company in a matter of seconds.

By giving a computer an appropriate set of instructions, it can very quickly perform a wide range of tasks. <u>A computer is a very fast working, but completely stupid, machine</u>.

Hardware and software

A personal computer is a complete system which can be placed on your desk. It can perform a whole range of tasks at very high speeds, but it needs two specific parts to make it work, *hardware* and *software*.

- ☮ **Hardware** is the physical components of a computer that you can see and touch, e.g. the screen, the keyboard, the printer and the system unit.

- ☮ **Software** is the programs that are run on your computer to turn it into something useful, e.g. word processing, spreadsheet, database and games programs.

A computer without programs is like a car without petrol or a television without an arial!

Hardware and software are discussed more fully in the following chapters.

What can a computer do?

The tasks which a computer performs can be broken down into four main categories as follows:

- ☮ Receive information

- ☮ Process information

- ☮ Send out information

- ☮ Store information

By information we mean text, numbers, pictures and even electrical voltages. It is the combination of these four processes, controlled with the help of programs, which allow computers to be so versatile.

Word processing, for example, is only a matter of recieving data via the keyboard, processing the data and sending it out to the screen and probably sending it out to a printer too. Finally, the document will probably be stored on a diskette or hard disk.

DOS and Windows

You have probably already seen and heard the words *DOS* and *Windows*
Both are discussed in more detail in a later chapter, but for now here is a
very brief explanation of what they are:

☺ **DOS** is a program that you must have running on your computer to
make it work, so it is loaded automatically when you start your computer. It controls many vital aspects of computing such as transferring information to and from diskettes and hard disks and allocating
memory space to your programs and data. DOS is often referred to
as a *system program* or an *operating system*.

☺ **Windows** is a more advanced operating system designed to make
using computers easier by presenting things graphically. The picture
below shows a typical Windows screen with icons that you can
click on.

Doubleclick
the icon to
start the
program

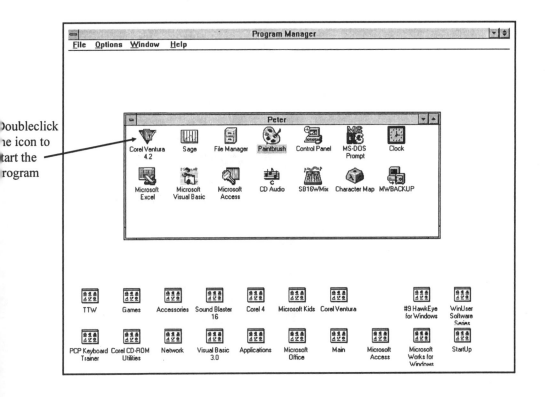

The Parts of a Computer

While their appearance varies, the basic parts which make up a personal computer are the same. All computers generally have the following:

- A keyboard to allow the user to give instructions or input information.

- A system unit that contains the processor, memory chips, video card, disk drive for diskettes (sometimes called floppy disks) and a hard disk.

- A screen (sometimes called a monitor or VDU) to show what's going on.

- A printer to printout documents and other files.

Most often the screen, system unit and keyboard will be separate units.

A *laptop* (portable computer) will have everything in one small unit.

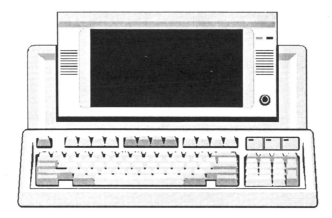

The keyboard

The keyboard has a layout that is similar to a typewriter, but it has several extra keys. It is used to send instructions to the computer and to input required information or data. Many beginners are slightly wary of pressing keys because they do not understand what happens. They're worried that they can in some way destroy data, or even the computer itself, if they press the wrong combination of keys. This is not the case, however.

The mouse

A mouse is a pointing object that can be used instead of, or in conjunction with the keyboard. It is particularly useful, and even necessary, when drawing with the computer, or creating printed matter (desk top publishing). A mouse will have two or three buttons which can be *clicked* and *doubleclicked*.

When you move the mouse across the table, a rubber ball on the under side of the mouse is rolled around, and its movement converted and conveyed to a pointer on the screen, which is moved in the same way as when you move the cursor with the cursor keys.

A more recent development, the trackball, is rather like an upside down mouse, where you use the palm of your hand to move the ball in the desired direction.

Optical mice also exist. In this case a light sensitive "eye" is moved around on a chequered mat.

There are of course different standards as far as mice are concerned and many mice can perform in different modes. However, all software that uses a mouse is compatible with a Microsoft mouse, so when choosing a mouse always make sure that it has a Microsoft mouse mode.

The screen

The screen, or monitor, is rather like a television set, although it does not function in quite the same way. Its display is the computer's way of showing you what's going on. It can also be referred to as the video display unit (VDU).

There are many kinds of screens, but the main difference is between *monochrome* models that can only display images in black and white, and *colour* monitors that can reproduce the full visual spectrum. Nearly all computers theses days have a colour screen.

The standard screen size is to 14", but large screens exist for special purposes. Technical drawings and production of books and documents often benefit from a 17" or 20" screen.

Older screens are usually *digital* screens. That means that each dot, or pixel, can be turned on or off. A grey colour is achieved by a group of pixels working together - the more pixels that are turned off, the darker the grey colour appears. Modern *analogue* screens can control the intensity of each dot, allowing a wide variety of colours and hues to be displayed.

Video cards and resolution

The screen is necessary for the computer to display its results, calculations, graphs, letters, etc. Information is fed to the screen via a *video card*, sometimes called a *graphics card*, which is installed inside the main system unit and connected to the screen. There are several different display standards and so the capabilities of the screen and video card need to be matched.

The resolution of the screen decides the quality of the picture that can be displayed. Each screen has a number of dots, or pixels, that can be illuminated and it is this configuration (e.g. 800 x 600 pixels) that is quoted on sales brochures and in advers, etc.

All screens can display a basic monochrome text display with 25 lines of 80 characters each. Most screens are capable of displaying one or more of the following graphics standards:

Type	Colour	Pixels
MDA	No	No graphics
HGA (Hercules)	No	740 x 380
CGA	Yes	320 x 200
EGA	Yes	640 x 350
VGA	Yes	640 x 480
SVGA (Super VGA)	Yes	800 x 600
UGA	Yes	1280 x 1024

The VGA and SVGA standards currently dominate the market.

Many video cards and screens are capable of displaying several standards. VGA and SVGA have, for example, a monochrome mode where grey shades can be displayed as well as the standard full colour mode.

A useful type of screen is a *Multisync* screen that can automatically swap to the graphic standard used by the program.

The latest video cards have a processor on them that reduces the work load of the main system processor and speeds up the process of showing graphics on the screen. This is vital for working with programs that have a heavy graphical content.

The system unit

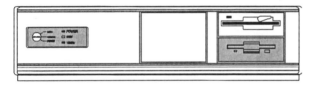

The system unit is the central part of a computer. All other units, like the monitor and the keyboard, are connected to, and controlled by, this unit. It contains many components such as the *motherboard* with the main *processor* and *memory chips*, the video card, a disk drive and a hard disk.

The components in the system unit process the input from your keyboard and control the output to your monitor.

The processor - 286, 386, 486, Pentium, etc.

While all computers can do essentially the same things, the speed at which they run depends on the processor they are built around as the processor controls all other components. There are several different processors and in order of effectiveness, with the slowest and most limited first, they are the 8086, 80286, 80386, 80846 and the Pentium (or 80586). The type of processor used is what gives the computer its name.

The first computers called PC's and XT's had 8086 or 8088 processors, then came the AT's with their 80286 processors. Today 386 and 486 machines, with 80386 and 80486 processors, are the most common. Super fast Pentium machines are becoming more popular.

Basically, each new processor in the chain provides more computing power.

Clock speeds - MHz

Each type of processor can work at different speeds. The speed at which a processor works is governed by its clock speed. On each tick of the clock the processor carries out an instruction, so the faster the clock is ticking the faster the processor cdoes its work.

Here are some common clock speeds given in MHz:

Processor	Typical clock speeds
8086, 8088	4.77, 10
80286	12, 16, 20
80386SX	16, 20, 25
80386	16, 20, 25, 33, 40
80486	25, 33, 50, 66
Pentium (80856)	55, 60

Clock speed is just one aspect affecting the overall speed of a system. A 80386 based system running at 33 MHz is typically only half as fast as a 80486 system running at a mere 25 MHz.

Multitasking

A major breakthrough came with the arrival of the 80386 based computers. These could run several programs at the same time, called multitasking, and simply swap between the programs with a few key strokes. A special program is, however, required to achieve this, the most popular being Windows.

SX and DX machines

To bring the price of a 386 computer down a special version of the standard 80386 processor, called the 386DX, was developed. Called a 386SX. it is a sort of "reduced version" of the 386DX.

You may be wondering what you lose out on with a 386SX. The answer is speed alone - a 386SX is in fact one and the same processor as an ordinary 386DX, but with fewer of its pins connected - it would have been too expensive to develop a new processor for the job.

486SXs are also common. This is basically the same as the standard 486DX, but with the internal co-processor removed (a 486 has one as an integral part of the processor!).

The computer's memory

An integral part of the system unit is the computer's memory, where text and numbers are stored. For example, a number can be stored in the computer's memory and retrieved later to be used in a multiplication operation.

There are two very different sorts of memory, ROM memory and RAM memory. These are described below.

ROM

ROM stands for Read Only Memory. It is a pre-programmed memory chip containing vital information for the computer to function. Read Only means that the data stored can only be read and not changed.

RAM

RAM stands for Random Access Memory. It is a volatile memory, that is it can store data, have the data wiped out and store new data. It is dependent on a current, so when you switch off the computer the contents of RAM memory disappears.

Bits and bytes

Bits and bytes are the actual units of memory. One byte is one unit of memory, a letter or a number. Each byte consists of 8 bits which can take the value of 0 or 1. The combination of 0's and 1's determines which character a byte of information represents.

1024 bytes of memory is the same as 1 kilobyte (kb). Thus a computer with 640 kb RAM has in effect 1024 x 640 = 65536 bytes or units of memory each capable of storing 1 character.

A 360 kb diskette can store just over 360000 characters, or around 200 pages of text.

Memory size and SIMM expansion modules

The size of your computer's memory is measured in bytes, or kilobytes. Each byte is the same as one character. For example, the text "How nice you are!" would take up 17 bytes, not forgetting the blanks and the exclamation mark. A kilobyte is 1024 bytes, and it's sometime just called *K*, or *Kb*.

The important thing, from the user's point of view, is the size of the computer's RAM type memory. Programs are loaded into RAM, and larger programs require larger RAM. If your computer's RAM is too small, you will not be able to run some of the larger programs.

Modern computers are supplied with at least 4 Mb of memory although some older computers may have as little as 640 kb, 1 Mb or 2 Mb. Computers used for graphics and desktop publishing will have 8 Mb, 16 Mb or even 32 Mb.

It is possible to increase the size of the memory by addingmore memory chips, called SIMM memory modules, which come in 1 Mb or 4 Mb modules. The system unit case is unplugged and the memory modules simply clipped into place in the available memory expansion slots.

Data storage

One of the most important aspects of a computer is its capability to store and recall information. When you are creating a document, for example, the text is stored in RAM, but this means that all information disappears when you turn the computer off. You can, however, make a copy of that information on a floppy disk or hard disk. This allows you, at a later time, to recall the stored information and load it into your computer again. You can then extend, edit or erase the document.

The whole of chapter 4 is dedicated to hard disks, diskettes and disk drives.

Printers

Printing is one of the main goals for computer users. Letters, accounts, graphs and pictures are some examples of why we use computers at all, so how to produce the final result becomes very important. In this section the different types of printers will be discussed briefly along with the most common printer problems that occur.

Types of printers

There are basically five types of printer:

- Dot matrix
  Ink jet
  Laser
  Plotter

Dot matrix printers

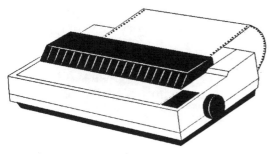

The most common and least expensive type of printer is the dot matrix printer. This works by hammering pins against a ribbon and the paper in such a pattern as to form the necessary characters.

There are several interesting points to note; the printing speed, the quality of the printout, the available types of printout and the standards it can emulate.

The printing speed is always quoted in characters per second, but this speed relates to the top speed that the printer can reach. In effect the average printing speed will be much lower when line breaks and the stop and start movements are taken into account. Thus a reasonably cheap dot matrix printer with a quoted print speed of 80 cps (characters per second) may only manage 40 on average.

A golden rule is; the higher the printing speed the higher the price. Some dot matrix printers have two or three printing heads thus increasing the printing speed up to 800 cps.

 The print quality is determined by the actual design of the printer and the number of pins used in the printing head. Many printers use 9 pins to form each character, while a more expensive printer uses 24 pins. It is easy to guess which is the more expensive, but you really can see the difference.

Dot matrix printers can normally print in compressed style (a smaller print than the standard), expanded style (double width print) and near letter quality (NLQ). NLQ printing gives a much better quality printout and slows the printing down considerably. More expensive printers offer even more possibilities.

As far as standards go, there are two important ones to note - one for text and one for graphics. The IBM Proprinter is such an important standard that virtually all dot matrix printers can emulate this standard, and virtually all software that uses a printer can be set-up for this standard. A similar standard exists for printing graphics - here the standard is EPSON FX. Dot matrix printers, are however, not ideally suited to working with graphics.

Many printers can also emulate other printers and even have their own "mode" or character set, but this is not definitely an advantage - for the user with more simple needs it is probably better to install the printer and programs to use the IBM standard.

Colour dot matrix printers are now available.

Laser printers

Laser printers give high speed, top quality printouts. Laser printers are the best printers available and have the highest price tag.

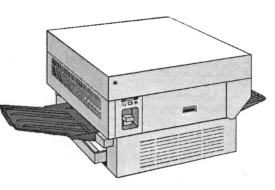

Laser printers print a whole page at a time. The speed of a laser printer is judged by the number of completed sheets it can turn out per minute. Typical "slow" lasers produce 4 pages per minute (ppm) others 6, 8, 10 or more ppm. The printing speed is, however, dependent on what you are printing - a page containing a large picture may take several minutes to print.

The quality of a laser printout is measured by the dots per inch (dpi) printed - like the dot matrix printer the laser printer in fact prints just a lot of dots! Most laser printers print at 300 dpi, thus a square inch will contain 300 x 300 = 90 000 dots. The latest models print at 600 dpi and the quality is good enough to produce master copies for manuals and books. One system at least can print at a staggering 1200 dpi, which is gives a quality equal to typesetting in the traditional manner.

There are some important standards for laser printers; HP Laser Jet and HP Graphics Language and PostScript. With HP compatible laser printers you get a few standard typefaces that can print in a different sizes, but can add special cartridges or typeface programs to extend the range of printing possibilities. High quality graphics can also be printed.

PostScript and laser printers

PostScript is a special page description language that can be used to print text and graphics. The characters that can be printed are scaleable. This means that rather than storing a copy of each character in different sizes as a pattern of dots, each character is described by the way it is formed. Thus the characters can be printed at any size, within the limits set by the printer. PostScript printers are often supplied with 35 different typefaces and others can be installed through special typeface programs.

Ink-jet printers

Ink-jet printers lie somewhere between dot matrix and laser printers. The quality is nearly as high as that of a laser printer and the price much lower. Ink-jet printers are quiet, cheap alternatives to dot matrix printers. The quality of the printout depends on how many dots are squirted onto the paper, rather like the number of pins in the printing head of a dot matrix.

Print speeds are comparable to dot matrix print speeds and thus much slower than laser printers. Unfortunately some ink-jet printers have their own standards, although many can emulate the all-important IBM Proprinter and EPSON standards. If you are considering buying such an ink-jet printer you must therefore check the standards each printer make can emulate, and check your software to see which standards it can be set up to use.

Plotters

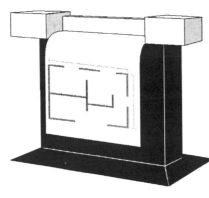

Plotters are a different sort of printing mechanism often associated with CAD/CAM and other drawing programs. The important difference is that plotters actually use pens that are steered around the paper to produce real lines rather than patterns of dots.

A typical plotter may have four, six or eight different colour pens. The higher the resolution the better the quality of the printout. Printing speed is also important as full page drawings can take a long time to be printed.

Finally, in the world of plotters, HP GL (Hewlett Packard Graphics Language) is the standard - the very same standard as used in some laser printers.

Printer standards and control codes

The last few pages have involved some talk of standards - here's why they are so important...

Let us assume that you wish to print the words "a million" in bold text. Apart from sending the actual words to the printer, the printer must be told that bold type is requested. Thus prior to the actual words a control code is sent to set up the printer for bold typing. The actual words are then sent and printed. Finally a new control code will be sent to the printer to mark the end of the bold printing. It is these control codes that constitute a standard.

For example, the IBM Proprinter standard requires two code numbers to activate bold type - 27 and then 69. Code number 27 is very special and represents Escape, this informs the printer that a control code is coming rather than ordinary text. 69 is the code number to start bold printing. After this the text "a million" is sent and printed. Finally the control numbers to end bold printing, 27 and 70, are sent to the printer. The IBM Proprinter standard covers a set of pre-defined control number sequences to control the printer.

Normally your word processor, or other program you are using, sends the necessary control codes to your printer. You will have marked a certain block of text as bold, for example, and the program does the rest. If your program is set up for a different standard it will probably send a completely different control code for bold printing, which will produce anything except the desired result!

Scanners

A scanner is used to digitise a picture so that the picture can then be used on your computers.

 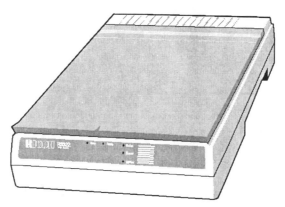

Modems

Modems are used to connect two computers for transferring data. The computers can be neer to each other or on the other side of the world.

Computer communications are discussed in a later chapter.

Multimedia

One of the fastest growing areas is that of multimedia. Multimedia is the ability to use sound and pictures on your computer. The components of a multimedia system are as follows:

☺ A CD-ROM drive for storage of large amounts of information

☺ A sound card and speakers to get stereo music out of your computer.

☺ If you have a video board you can capture actual video shots from a video recorder or camera.

Multimedia systems certainly offer the possibility of turning your computer into something special. Computer games become exceptional and large reference works can give you masses of information, pictures, video clips and authentic sounds.

Programs are supplied on CDs which are just like the musical CDs. In fact a comuter can play musical CDs so you can have music while you work!

Your Keyboard Explained

When confronted with a computer keyboard for the first time, novices are often frightened by the many keys other than the normal typewriter keys. The mysterious symbols and the complexity of the keyboard, do require some explanation. This chapter describes how your keyboard works and explains some important keys you may not be familiar with.

How your keyboard works

Your computer is continually checking to see if any key has been pressed. In fact, a computer spends most of its time idly waiting for you to press a key! Each time you do press a key a special code for that key is generated. The code is then 'picked up' by the computer and sent to the main processor to be processed. This will often involve displaying a letter on the screen, or reacting to a selected menu or option choice.

The keyboard has its own small *buffer*, or memory, to store the keystrokes you make. If the computer is busy, the keystrokes will be held in the buffer until the computer is ready to process them. If the buffer gets filled up the computer will beep to inform you that the keyboard cannot accept any more keystrokes.

Keys normally have an auto-repeat function. This means that if you keep a key depressed, the computer will see this as if you are repeatedly pressing that key and the buffer may soon fill up.

Different keyboards

Although there are several different keyboard models, there are two main layouts. These days nearly all keyboards have a line of function keys, marked **F1 - F12**, in a row along the top of the keyboard. Older keyboards have a group of function keys **F1 - F10** in pairs down the left-hand side of the keyboard.

Alphanumerical keys

 The alphanumerical keys are the normal letters and numbers, **A**, **B**, **C**, **1**, **2**, **3**, etc., as found on a standard typewriter.

The Shift keys

 Upper case letters and the characters over the number keys, **!**, **"**, **£**, etc., are obtained by pressing the **Shift** key in conjunction with the desired key. There are two **Shift** keys, one on the left-hand side and one on the right-hand side of the bottom row of letters. There is no difference between the two **Shift** keys - sometimes you use one, sometimes the other, depending on which other key you are also pressing.

Combined numerical keypad and cursor movement keys

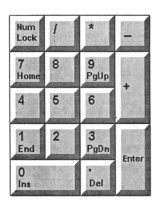 On a modern keyboard there is a special numerical keypad on the right-hand side of the keyboard. These keys can function in two ways, depending on the state of the Number Lock function.

By pressing the **NumLock** key, the **NumLock** lamp above the keypad will be turned on and off.

Num Lock indicator on
With NumLock lamp lit, these keys will work as number keys.

Num Lock indicator off
With NumLock lamp not lit, these keys will work as cursor movement keys.

Separate cursor movement keys

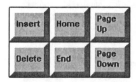 Some keyboards will have a separate group of keys dedicated to cursor movement. Just how, and if, they work, will depend on the program you are running.

Home. This key is often used to move the cursor to the beginning of a line, screen display, or text.

End. This key is often used to move the cursor to the end of a line, screen display, or text.

Page Up. This key is often used to move the cursor to the beginning of a screen display, or text.

Page Down. This key is often used to move the cursor to the end of screen display, or text.

Insert. This key is often used to control how new text is inserted into a text. Pressing the key will often toggle between an insert and overwrite mode. Insert means that text will be inserted at the cursor's position and the following text moved over. The overwrite mode will cause text entered at the cursor's position to replace that which already exists.

Delete. This key is often used to delete the character at the cursor's position.

The Arrow keys

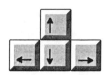 The **Arrow** keys are most often used to move the cursor one position in the indicated direction.

Function keys

The function keys are grouped in a row at the top of the keyboard (modern keyboards, **F1-F12)** or on the left-hand side of the keyboard (older keyboards, **F1-F10)** .

These keys are used by application programs, and will be assigned different functions for each program, and sometimes different functions at different points within the same program. Think of these as "short cut" keys, since they are usually used to let one keystroke do the job of many.

For example, **F1** is often used to call up a help screen (especially in Windows' programs), but could also be used to save a text in a word processor program, or to delete an entry in a database program. In each case, without the use of the function key, you might have to perform several different commands to make the program do what you want.

Special keys

This section covers some of the keys with a special importance.

Enter key

The **Enter** key is perhaps the most important key of all. There are usually two **Enter** keys, one to the right of the alphanumerical, or typewriter, keys, and one on the numerical keypad. **Enter** is mainly used in two ways.

⊕   When typing in commands, instructions, and data, you usually have to press **Enter** key to confirm your input. In such cases, although you may have typed in a command, it is not processed until you have pressed the **Enter** key.

⊕   A word processor program (and other programs involving entering text) will require you to press the **Enter** key to mark the end of a paragraph, and move the cursor down to the next line. This is similar to the CR (Carriage Return) key of a standard typewriter.

Backspace key

 The **Backspace** key is normally used to delete the character immediately to the left of the cursor.

Caps Lock key

 This key is used to lock the alphabetical keys, **A-Z**, to their upper-cases, as for a standard typewriter. The **Shift** key is then used to produce lower-case letters.

Ctrl key

 The **Ctrl** key (short for Control) is used together with other keys, e.g. **Ctrl+B**, **Ctrl+End**, to perform special operations in an application program.

Alt key

 The **Alt** (short for Alternative) key is also used together with other keys, e.g. **Alt+F5**, **Alt+U**, to perform special operations in an application program. It can also be used in conjunction with the numerical keypad, it's used to print special characters on the screen. More information about this is given at the end of this chapter together with a list of available characters.

Esc key

 The **Esc** key (short for Escape) is usually used in application programs to exit a part of that program, close a menu or undo a change you have made.

Tab key

 This key is normally used to jump between pre-defined margin positions, or between input fields in a database.

Print Screen key

 This key will result in a copy of the screen display being sent to the printer for printing, or when using Windows, the copy being sent to the Clipboard.

Producing graphics characters with the Alt key

Your computer is not only capable of producing letters and numbers, it can also produce many graphic characters. These characters can be used with certain programs, for example, to create boxes and lines.

To write these characters, which are not displayed on any of the keys on your keyboard, you need to press the **Alt** key, in conjunction with a number code, using the number keys on the right-hand side of the keyboard.

To obtain a character in the table, you must look up its ASCII number code. The example below will type an Ä character.

- Hold down the **Alt** key.

- Type in the code number for the desired character, using the number key pad on the right-hand side of the keyboard, for example:

  142

- Release the **Alt** key.

☞ *This will not necessarily work for all programs or printers, since some use their own character sets. In such cases, you should consult the appropriate manual.*

The ASCII table

The ASCII Table shows the number and corresponding character of the IBM character set. These are the characters you can print using the **Alt** key.

☞ *If you are running Windows, a different character set is used and different characters will be produced in some cases.*

21 = §	69 = E	107 = k	145 = æ	183 = ⊓	221 = ▌	
32 =	70 = F	108 = l	146 = Æ	184 = ╕	222 = ▐	
33 = !	71 = G	109 = m	147 = ô	185 = ╣	223 = ▀	
34 = "	72 = H	110 = n	148 = ö	186 = ║	224 = α	
35 = #	73 = I	111 = o	149 = ò	187 = ╗	225 = β	
36 = %	74 = J	112 = p	150 = û	188 = ╝	226 = Γ	
37 =	75 = K	113 = q	151 = ù	189 = ╜	227 = π	
38 = &	76 = L	114 = r	152 = ÿ	190 = ╛	228 = Σ	
39 = ´	77 = M	115 = s	153 = Ö	191 = ┐	229 = σ	
40 = (	78 = N	116 = t	154 = Ü	192 = └	230 = µ	
41 =)	79 = O	117 = u	155 = ¢	193 = ┴	231 = τ	
42 = *	80 = P	118 = v	156 =	194 = ┬	232 = Φ	
43 = +	81 = Q	119 = w	157 = ¥	195 = ├	233 = θ	
44 = ,	82 = R	120 = x	158 = ₧	196 = ─	234 = Ω	
45 = –	83 = S	121 = y	159 = ƒ	197 = ┼	235 = δ	
46 = .	84 = T	122 = z	160 = á	198 = ╞	236 = ∞	
47 = /	85 = U	123 = {	161 = í	199 = ╟	237 = ø	
48 = 0	86 = V	124 = ┃	162 = ó	200 = ╚	238 = ∈	
49 = 1	87 = W	125 = }	163 = ú	201 = ╔	239 = ∩	
50 = 2	88 = X	126 = ~	164 = ñ	202 = ╩	240 = ≡	
51 = 3	89 = Y	127 = ⌂	165 = Ñ	203 = ╦	241 = ±	
52 = 4	90 = Z	128 = Ç	166 = ª	204 = ╠	242 = ≥	
53 = 5	91 = [	129 = ü	167 = º	205 = ═	243 = ≤	
54 = 6	92 = \	130 = é	168 = ¿	206 = ╬	244 = ⌠	
55 = 7	93 =]	131 = â	169 = ⌐	207 = ╧	245 = ⌡	
56 = 8	94 = ^	132 = ä	170 = ¬	208 = ╨	246 = ÷	
57 = 9	95 = _	133 = à	171 = ½	209 = ╤	247 = ≈	
58 = :	96 = `	134 = å	172 = ¼	210 = ╥	248 = °	
59 = ;	97 = a	135 = ç	173 = ¡	211 = ╙	249 = ●	
60 = <	98 = b	136 = ê	174 = «	212 = ╘	250 = ·	
61 = =	99 = c	137 = ë	175 = »	213 = ╒	251 = √	
62 = >	100 = d	138 = è	176 = ░	214 = ╓	252 = ⁿ	
63 = ?	101 = e	139 = ï	177 = ▒	215 = ╫	253 = ²	
64 = @	102 = f	140 = î	178 = ▓	216 = ╪	254 = ■	
65 = A	103 = g	141 = ì	179 = │	217 = ┘	255 =	
66 = B	104 = h	142 = Ä	180 = ┤	218 = ┌		
67 = C	105 = i	143 = Å	181 = ╡	219 = █		
68 = D	106 = j	144 = É	182 = ╢	220 = ▄		

Data Storage

One of the most important aspects of a computer is its capability to store and recall information. When you are creating a document, for example, the text is stored in RAM, but this means that all information disappears when you turn the computer off. You can, however, make a copy of that information on a floppy disk or hard disk. This allows you, at a later time, to recall the stored information and load it into your computer again. You can then extend, edit or erase the document.

Data can be stored on:

☻ Diskettes (floppy disks)
  Hard disks
  Magnetic tape
  Optical disks
  CDs

Diskettes

Diskettes, sometimes referred to as floppies or floppy disks, are small plastic wafers covered with a magnetic particles that are used for storing information. There are two main sizes of diskettes, 3.5" and 5.25" disks, which refer to the actual diameter of the disks in inches.

Each diskette can store a certain amount of bytes of information, but this does not depend on the physical size of the disk.

☻ A 3.5" diskette can store 720 kb.

☻ A high-density (HD) 3.5" diskette can store 1.44 Mb.

☺ A 5.25" diskette can store 360 kb.

☺ A high-density (HD) 5.25" diskette can store 1.2 Mb.

As an example, a 360 kb disk can store the equivalent of about 200 pages of printed text.

Diskettes can be moved between computers, assuming that both computers are IBM compatible and have the same kind of disk drives. You can, for example, create a text on your computer at work, save a copy of that text on a diskette, and take it home with you for use on your computer at home.

Look after your diskettes

A diskette is a very thin magnetised plastic wafer surrounded by a plastic housing. You can damage a diskette and lose everything that is stored on it. In particular, diskettes are sensitive to:

☺ Temperature
   Magnets
   Water

☺ 5.25" diskettes should not be bent

Don't put a diskette on or near anything that has a large magnet!

Write-protecting disks

Write-protection is a way of preventing your computer from writing data onto a disk, thereby avoiding the possibility of damaging other data on the disk. This is really only a very small risk, but if it happens to you just once, with a disk full of your most precious writings or figures...!

The two main uses for write-protection are to protect your MASTER disks and to protect disks which contain important information, such as archive copies of documents and statistics, from being accidentally erased.

5.25" disks

A 5.25" disk has a write-protect notch on the right-hand side, if you hold it with the front of the disk facing you (label at top if there is one).

⊕ To write protect the disk, cover the notch with one of the labels that come with every box of new disks, or with a piece of opaque tape.

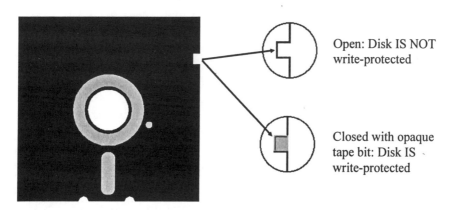

Open: Disk IS NOT write-protected

Closed with opaque tape bit: Disk IS write-protected

With the write-protect notch covered, your computer will not be able to write any data on the disk. It will, however, still be able to read the existing data so that you can use or make copies of the files on it.

⊕ To un-protect the disk, remove any tape that covers the notch.

3.5" disks

A 3.5" disk has a square write-protect hole with a sliding tab on the right-hand side, if you hold it with the front of the disk facing you and the tab on the reverse side.

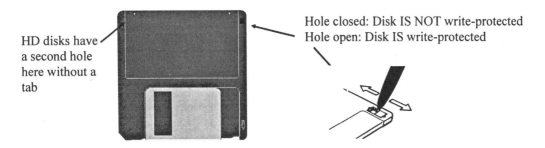

HD disks have a second hole here without a tab

Hole closed: Disk IS NOT write-protected
Hole open: Disk IS write-protected

⊕ To write-protect the disk, move the tab, so that there is a hole right through the disk.

With the write-protect tab open, your computer will not be able to write any data on the disk. It will, however, still be able to read the existing data, so that you can use and make copies of the files on it.

⊕ To un-protect the disk again, move the tab so that the hole is blocked.

Disk drives

The use of diskettes requires a disk drive. This is a unit that reads and records information on diskettes. It's normally mounted in the system unit, although it is possible to have a free-standing unit. All computers have at least one such disk drive and some have two.

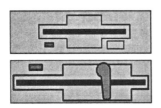

To use a diskette, you just insert the disk into the available slot. Most 5.25" units also require you to push a lever or door down to enable it to function properly.

Hard disks

A hard disk is a rigid set of disks that are mounted permanently within the system unit. A hard disk can store much more information than a diskette and also works much faster.

Although it is possible to remove a hard disk drive and install it in another computer, it is very unusual to move hard disks around between computers. Having said this, it is worth mentioning there are also portable hard disk drives, which use specially designed cases to make it easy to remove and refit them. A hard disk is a set of disks, with multiple *read and write heads* that allow it to store and access very large amounts of data very quickly. A small hard disk can store 40 Mb of data, which is the equivalent of about 20,000 pages of text. Larger hard disks can store over 600 Mb. If you are running Windows a 200 Mb hard disk is preferable.

A computer that has a hard disk is much better equipped than one that doesn't have a hard disk. Many larger programs now require a hard disk: and, since they operate three to ten times faster than floppy drive, their use is habit forming.

ABC for disk drives

Your computer will automatically give a name to each of the disk drives in your system. The letters A:, B:, C: etc. are used. This is done so that it is possible to keep track of which drive the computer is working with.

- The first diskette drive is called drive A:.
- The second diskette drive is called drive B:.
- The first hard disk drive is called drive C:, even if you do not have a diskette drive named B:.
- Subsequent disk drives are named D:, E:, F:, etc.

The current drive

Your computer may have just one disk drive, or two, or one or two plus a hard disk, or more than one hard disk, and so on. As mentioned earlier, each drive will be given its own name, such as A:, B:, C:, etc.

When working with DOS commands, you will always be doing something with a file in a specific drive. DOS commands will involve a drive name, and a filename. The concept of a current drive, however, provides a useful short cut. In fact it is a little more complicated than that, because if you make a mistake, DOS can assume, for example, that you wanted to do something with a file on the current drive, when really you meant another drive, but forgot to name it.

The current drive concept is very important to grasp. A normal DOS command, with a specified drive and filename, can be shortened to only a filename, whereupon DOS will assume that the omission of the drive name means that the current drive name is to be used by default. Some exercises which follow later on in this book will use this concept.

You can change the current drive, when the system prompt is shown, by just typing in the drive letter, followed by a colon (:), and then pressing the **Enter** key.

> **a:**   will change the current drive to drive A
> **b:**   will change the current drive to drive B.
> **c:**   will change the current drive to drive C.

More about disks

A disk is a thin round plastic disc coated with a very thin film containing millions of magnetic particles. Data is stored on the diskette by magnetising these particles. The particles are arranged in a number of tracks, or concentric rings, on both sides of the diskette.

When you buy a new diskette or hard disk has no data stored on it, just a number of empty concentric tracks. Furthermore, DOS requires the all disks to be divided into small areas (sectors) that are easy to work with. Thus a new disk has to be prepared for use, this is called formatting. Even used disks with information stored on them can be formatted. This results in all stored data being wiped out as the disk is re-formatted.

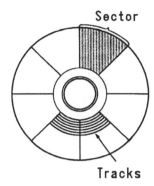

Sector

Tracks

For a standard 5.25" diskette each track is divided up into 9 segments, or sectors, each storing 512 bytes of data. Thus a standard 5.25" diskette with 40 tracks per side would be able to store 40 tracks x 9 sectors x 512 x 2 sides = 368 640 bytes.

There are two diskette sizes, the old standard 5.25" and the new standard 3.5". The 3.5" diskettes have taken over because of their smaller format, they can store more information than the 5.25" diskettes, and because the hard plastic casing offers far better protection than their floppy 5.25" counterparts.

Hard disks are similarly divided into tracks and sectors. The number of disks and read/write heads will also vary.

Disk organisation

When you format a disk, DOS divides that disk into four different areas, the *boot record*, the *File Allocation Table* (FAT), the *root directory*, and the *data area*. Note that the following explanations also apply for a hard disk.

The outside track, nearest the outside edge, is known as track 0. The first sector of the first track is called sector 1.

The boot record

The boot record occupies sector 1 of track 0 on a disk. It contains a short program that in its turn reads the system files necessary to start the computer. It also contains some vital information about the disk itself. This information is so important that it is written to all disks, even those that are not system disks.

FAT (File Allocation Table)

The FAT maintains information on each sector of the disk - whether it is data is stored in a particular sector or if the sector is free to be used. When formatting a disk all sectors are tested by DOS and any faulty sectors are marked as 'bad' in the FAT thus making sure that the sector is not used to store information.

The root directory

Formatting a disk also creates a root directory. Here information is stored on each file found on the diskette - the filename and its extension, the date and time of its creation, the size of the file and where on the diskette the program starts.

The data area

The fourth and final area of a disk is the data area, which takes up the rest of the disk space. It is used to store data - programs and data files, and information on any subdirectories created.

Diskette storage capacity

Both 5.25" and 3.5" diskettes have two different types of diskette which can store differing amounts of data.

There are standard diskettes (often called double density or DD) and high-density diskettes (HD). The following table shows how much each size and type of diskette can store.

Size	Type	Storage capacity
5.25"	standard (DD)	360 kb
5.25"	high-density (HD)	1.2 Mb (1,200 kb)
3.5"	standard (DD)	720 kb
3.5"	high-density (HD)	1.44 Mb (1,440 kb)

The higher capacities are enabled by cramming more information onto each diskette. For example, you have already read that a standard 5.25" diskette has 40 tracks x 9 sectors per track x 512 bytes per sector x 2 side = approx. 360 kb. A high-density 5.25" diskette has 80 tracks x 15 sectors x 512 bytes x 2 sides = approx. 1200 kb or 1.2 Mb.

Each type of diskette reserves space for the boot area, the FAT and the root directory decreasing slightly the space free to store programs and data. Furthermore a system diskette will also contain important system files that reduce the free space even more.

1 kb = 1024 bytes

If you do any calculations on storage capacities you may be slightly confused by the numbers not matching up exactly. This is because the computer world is governed by the binary system and 2x2x2x2x2x2x2x2x2x2=1024. Thus 1 kb is equated to 1024 bytes and 360 kb therefore becomes 360x1024=368 640 bytes.

More about hard disks

In many ways, a hard disk is like a floppy disk or diskette. It has the same boot record, FAT, root directory and data area. Rather than being a single disc, a hard disk is a closed unit housing several discs and many read/write heads. The unit is sealed to keep out dust which would affect the high precision workings.

Mass storage

The first hard disks could store no more than 5 or 10 Mb, which at the time was considered to be a lot. These days you cannot even buy such small hard disks, and some larger programs are so large that they would not fit onto such disks at all.

Hard disks have become mass storage units - 40 Mb, 80 Mb, 100 Mb, 200 Mb, 650 Mb are some examples of storage capacities. A 650 Mb hard disk is capable of storing the equivalent of over 300 000 standard text pages - that's some book! Why should anyone need such a large storage capacity? Obviously such a hard disk would be useful if shared by several users as in a network, for example. Graphics also often require large storage areas - a typical picture may use anything up to 1 Mb of storage space. A 40 Mb disk with perhaps 20 Mb free for storing pictures would soon be filled.

Access times

One of the major developments of hard disks is the average access time. This is the average time it takes to access any data anywhere on the disk and has become an important part of the overall performance of a computer system. Very slow hard disks have an average access time of around 65 ms (65 milliseconds, or 65/1000 of a second). Medium fast hard disks have access times of around 30 ms while faster hard disks take under 20 ms. This figure is continually being improved upon.

How does the average access time affect you? If you are using a program that does not read from or write to the hard disk, then the speed of the hard disk will only affect how fast the program is loaded in the first place - it may make a difference of a few seconds. On the other hand, a program that writes to and reads from the hard disk during its execution will be affected each and every time such an operation occurs. A slower hard disk here will keep you waiting a second or two longer each time.

The overall performance of the hard disk is, however, not solely a matter of access speeds. The so-called interleave and the rate of data transfer to the processor both play an important role.

Interleaves

Imagine that your computer needs to pick up some data from a single track on the hard disk. This track, and every other track, is divided into a number of sectors, typically seventeen. The fact is that a hard disk spins so fast that the computer cannot keep up with it. Reading the sectors one after the other as they spin past is too much for all but the fastest systems.

Let's assume that for each spin of the disk the computer can cope with reading one sector. Thus, to read all seventeen sectors, it would take seventeen disk revolutions, and the interleave factor is 17:1. Let's assume now that the computer can manage to read 5 sectors per revolution - interleave factor 5:1 - this would mean that four revolutions were necessary to read all 17 sectors. Reading every other sector (interleave factor 2:1) would require only 2 revolutions, the first revolution reading sectors 1, 3, 5, etc., with the second revolution reading sectors 2, 4, etc.

A standard PC with an 8088 processor will typically have an interleave factor of 5:1, and an AT a factor of 3:1. Changing the interleave factor is a way of tuning your hard disk performance to that of your computer, but not something for the beginner to tamper with!

Interface standards and Controller cards

The interface is the means of transferring the data read from a hard disk to the computer itself. It is known as a *Controller card*, and is an add-in card that is installed in the computer. All hard disks (and diskette drives) need a controller card.

The most common standard today is called IDE. In recent years other standards have been developed; SCSI (Small Computer System Interface) and ESDI (Enhanced Small Device Interface).

MFM and RLL

MFM (Modified Frequency Modulation) is the standard technique used for storing data on a disk. RLL (Run Length Limited) is a more recent technique for storing data that increases the capacity by up to 50%. It enables each track to be divided into 26 sectors instead of the normal 17. This increase affects the interleave ratio because the sectors are more tightly packed.

Some companies have started selling separate RLL hard disk controller cards, but be warned... It is not just a matter of replacing your standard MFM controller card with an RLL card and expecting a 50% increase. Because RLL increases the quantity of data stored it also needs a higher quality disk and most standard disks will not satisfy this need.

The 32 Mb limit

The rapid increase in storage capacities has caused problems. DOS was limited to using 32 Mb hard disks, although from DOS version 4.0 and later this limit has now been increased.

Partitions

If you have a DOS version earlier than 4.0 and a large hard disk, the hard disk must be divided into smaller units called partitions. For example, a 60 Mb hard disk may be divided up into two drives (C: and D:) each 30 Mb.

Thus, even though you only physically have one hard disk in your computer, the computer treats it as two separate hard disks.

Partitioning is done with the DOS command FDISK. Many computer dealers configure hard disks for you so that you will not need to use FDISK. If not, you will need to check out your DOS manual.

Hard disk cards

A hard disk card is an add-in card that is a hard disk and controller card all in one. It is a simple way of adding a hard disk to your computer, but will often take up a lot of room inside the computer. It requires a free expansion slot and will probably encroach upon the space for the adjacent card.

Other storage methods

Tape streamer

Anyone working with important information should consider it necessary to take back-up copies of their work. This should be done at regular intervals - even daily for companies with large amounts of information being processed.

The cheapest way of backing up your work is with the help of the DOS command BACKUP, or with a special back-up program, by copying your files onto diskettes. If you have small amounts of work to back up this is fine. Anyone who has done this knows that backing up even a small 40 Mb hard disk once a week becomes a tedious job.

Special back up tape units, or tape streamer, can be bought and programmed to take back-ups automatically, for example during your lunch hour. The initial investment becomes well worthwhile for anyone with serious amounts of data to back up.

Most people get round to thinking about back-ups when it is already too late. A hard disk crash, or just several important files destroyed or even accidentally erased - it is too late. Be wise and think about your needs now.

Optical disks

Optical disks have now been developed that can store 30 Mb and up to 200 Mb on one disk. Both the drives and the disks are special, you cannot use a standard disk drive or diskette.

CD ROM and WORM

CD ROM is destined to take over as a mass storage medium. CD stands for compact disk and is exactly the same as the musical CD records. In fact a CD ROM drive fitted to your computer can also play music!

The big advantage is the massive storage possibility - 600 Mb on one disk. Perfect for picture libraries, encyclopaedias, spelling checkers in several languages, collections of handbooks, library systems, etc. All of these applications already exist in reality.

As the name suggests, CD ROM is a read only system. You buy a pre-programmed diskette and cannot change the data on it. This is a major drawback but a WORM technique is being developed. WORM stands for Write Once Read Many. This means you buy an empty disk and can save data on it once, this data becoming permanently etched onto the disk.

Disk problems

The remainder of this chapter is dedicated to problems you may have with your hard disk including fragmentation that results in a considerable drop in performance. Don't worry if you do not understand everything at this point, you can always come back to this section if the need arises.

Computer does not boot from hard disk

If you turn on your computer (assuming you have a hard disk) and it refuses to start, then you have a serious problem. It may be caused by a DOS system file or the COMMAND.COM file being corrupt or even the CONFIG.SYS or AUTOEXEC.BAT files trying to run a corrupt file. Whatever the cause you cannot start your computer or access your files.

In such a case you will need a system diskette. By inserting the diskette in drive A and re-starting the computer you should at least get things going.

When the A:> prompt is displayed you can try to access the hard disk:

- Type:

    c:

- Press **Enter**.

If this does not succeed and you are faced with the message Invalid drive specification you have problems, and should seek the help of a knowledge-able person or try Norton Utilities (or a similar program) which is a software package specifically designed for data recovery and disk management. You could as a temporary measure check the cables from the controller card to the hard disk to see that they have not loosened.

If you successfully get the C:\> prompt you should rename the AUTO-EXEC.BAT and CONFIG.SYS files and try rebooting the computer to see if the fault lies here. Use the following commands:

    ren config.sys cfg.sys

    ren autoexec.bat ae.bat

If the computer successfully reboots then you know that the problem comes from one of these two files. If not then a DOS message, sometimes displayed when starting the computer, may help you.

Non-system disk suggests that the system files on your hard disk may have been damaged. Run the DOS command SYS to re-copy these to your hard disk as follows:

- Start your computer with a system diskette and then insert your DOS diskette in drive A.

- Type:

    sys c:

- Press **Enter**.

Bad or Missing Command Interpreter - this message implies that the system file COMMAND.COM is missing or has been damaged. Proceed as follows:

- Start your computer with a system diskette and then insert your DOS diskette in drive A.

- Type:

    copy command.com c:

- Press **Enter**.

If none of these solve the problem then you really need Norton Utilities or other suitable help.

Hard disk slowing down - fragmentation

When DOS saves your files on disk, it does not automatically save them as one long unit. Generally speaking, each file is divided into smaller units that fill one sector each on the hard disk. DOS will then fill in unused sectors anywhere on the disk so that one file may be spread out over a number of undetached sectors. From the beginning files will be saved in one long run, but as you save, overwrite and delete files more and more "holes" will appear on the disk and future files will be split - this is called fragmentation.

The net result of fragmentation is a slower hard disk. To read in a fragmented file the read/write head will have to be repositioned several times, so you will even hear the effects of loading and writing fragmented files.

Compression/Optimisation

The cure for fragmentation is disk compression or optimisation. You can buy a program, like PC Tools, that will reorganise your disk for you. It will read all the files on the disk and re-save them so that each file is stored as one long string of data on the disk, thus restoring data transfer speeds to their highest rate.

Disk compression is a quick and simple process and highly recommended for any serious hard disk user.

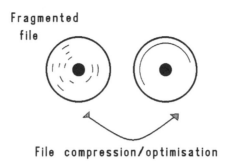

Fragmented
file

File compression/optimisation

Accidentally erased files

One thing that every computer user does at least once in his life is to mistakenly erase a wanted file or group of files. Erased files are often recoverable. Several programs are available that will help you to recover deleted files - PC Tools and Norton Utilities being two of the most popular.

When you erase a file DOS does not actually delete the data from the disk, it only replaces the first letter of the filename in the directory listing to mark the fact that the file is no longer in use. However, DOS will at some point use the freed space to save other files at which point the old deleted file is truly lost. If you discover that you have erased the wanted file early enough, you may well be able to recover it. To give yourself as much chance as possible of saving the file STOP WORKING with your computer - each time a file is saved you run the risk of deleting the old file for ever. Then run a file recovery program.

Accidentally formatted diskette

Sorry you're out of luck here. If you have accidentally formatted a diskette that contained vital data by using the DOS command FORMAT then the whole of the data area will have been wiped out.

Norton Utilities has a program called SF (Safe Format) that allows you to format diskettes without destroying the data area. Using this instead of the normal DOS command will mean that you can recover data from a re-formatted diskette. PC Tools offers a similar program PCFORMAT.

Accidentally formatted hard disk

Believe it or not there is a chance of recovering from an accidentally formatted hard disk, something that is a real threat for users with earlier DOS versions (later DOS versions will not format a hard disk without the disk name C:, D:, etc. being given, thus minimising the risk of accidental format). Again PC Tools/Norton Utilities offers help.

Read/write errors

Read/write errors occur when a sector has a bad CRC (Cyclic Redundancy Check). When information is written to a diskette a special checksum value is calculated and stored along with the data itself. When the data is read at a later date a new checksum is also calculated. The new checksum is compared with the checksum stored for that sector. If the two checksums do not match up then the data that was read from the disk is not the same as the data that was stored on the disk - a read error has occurred.

Most often this will mean that the program is unusable. If it is a data file you may or may not be able to salvage some of the data. Again PC Tools/Norton Utilities will be needed.

Filenames and Wildcards

One very important aspect of DOS is learning what you can call files - DOS has very specific rules about this! This chapter also deals with another important concept, that of *wildcards*, which provide you with a method of working with groups of files, or searching for a file when you are uncertain of the exact filename.

Filenames

You will, no doubt, already have seen a few filenames, on your computer or referred to in a manual perhaps. It is now time to give you the rules for filenames.

☺ A filename can be composed of two parts, the actual name and its extension.

☺ The name is one to eight characters in length.

☺ The extension, if it exists, is a period followed by one to three characters.

☞ *The new Windows v4, code named Chicago, will change this basic rule so that longer filenames can be used.*

All the following are examples of filenames:

FILE	FILE.EXE	FILE.DOC
TEST.L	TEST.TXT	TEST.COM
XYZ	X132.11	XR2TH76.HU

Upper and lower case

It makes no difference to DOS whether you use upper or lower case letters, or mix the two. Thus, the following filenames are equivalent:

File.TXT
FILE.TXT
file.txt
fILe.TXt.

Characters to avoid

Do not use the following characters in a filename:

- space
  exclamation mark (!)
  single quote (')
  double quotes (")
  dollar sign ($)
  plus sign (+)
  asterisk (*)
  less than symbol (<)
  greater than symbol (>)
  equals sign (=)
  slash (/)
  semi-colon (;)
  colon (:)
  comma (,)
  ampersand (&)
  the @ symbol

Naming files

As a rule, filenames should be relevant to the contents of the file. A file named WKI8Y7, will not help anyone to remember what it is, whereas names such as ORDER12.TXT, ORDER13.TXT, etc., give a hint to their contents. This may not seem important in the beginning, but with time you may well have hundreds of files so why not make it easy for yourself?

Common extension names

Some extensions are accepted standards, for example:

.EXE and .COM	are program files
.TXT	are text files
.DOC	are word processing files
.BAT	are batch files

Wildcards

The term wildcard is, perhaps, a strange term for the high technology computer world. But just as a joker can be used in place of another playing card in many card games, a wildcard can be used in DOS to substitute for any part of a filename.

Wildcards can be used together with many DOS commands, such as DIR, COPY, and DEL, where a filename has to be specified. They allow you to .specify groups of files, instead of just single files as we have done so far.

There are two different wildcards, each of which is explained below.

The ? wildcard

When specifying a filename, you can replace any of the characters in that name with a question mark (?). As an example, assume that you have the following files on your disk in drive B:

        TEST1.DOC
        TEST2.DOC
        FILEQ

Assume also that you want to delete the two files TEST1.DOC and TEST2.DOC. You could delete them one at a time with the following two commands:

        del b:test1.doc
        del b:test2.doc

The ? wildcard allows you, however, to delete both files simultaneously with the following command:

        del b:test?.doc

When your computer executes this, or any relevant command, it will match all files which exactly agree with the specified name, but which have any character instead of the ?. It would, therefore, delete TEST1.DOC and TEST2.DOC.

Assume now that you have the following files on your disk in drive B:

TEST1.DOC
TEST2.DOC
TEST3.DOC
TEST4.TXT
FILEQ

Now suppose that you want to delete TEST1.DOC, TEST2.DOC, and TEST4.TXT, but not TEST3.DOC. The same command, that is:

del b:test?.doc

would not be appropriate, on two accounts. First, TEST1.DOC and TEST2.DOC would be successfully deleted, but so would TEST3.DOC, which you didn't want to delete. Second, TEST4.TXT would not be deleted, because the extension part of the filename (.TXT), does not match the specified extension (.DOC). In this case, you would have to revert to deleting the files one at a time.

*The * wildcard*

The * wildcard is more powerful than the ? wildcard. A * in the specified filename can take the place of any character string. You are allowed to have one * wildcard in the first part of the filename, and one * wildcard in the extension part of the name. In each part of the filename, nothing must follow the wildcard - MYFI*.DOC is OK, MYFI*1.DOC isn't, M*.D* is OK, M*01.*D isn't.

Assume now that you have the following files on your disk in drive B:

TEST1.DOC
TEST1.BAK
TEST3.DOC
TEST4.TXT
FILEQ.BAK

Assume also, that you want to delete both files with the extension, .BAK, which generally means a back-up or duplicate file. You can do this with one command, as follows:

del b:*.bak

The * can be replaced by any filename, and the only important criteria is that the extension .BAK matches.

Now assume that you have the following files on your disk in drive B:

> TEST1.DOC
> TEST1.BAK
> TEST3.DOC
> TEST4.TXT
> FILEQ.BAK

Assume this time that you want to delete all files named TEST something, irrespective of their following number or extension. You can do this with one command, as follows:

> del b:t*.*

You are now telling the computer to delete all files that begin with a T (remember that the case of a filename is irrelevant) and have any extension.

*The *.* file specification*

Giving the filename specification *.* is extremely powerful. You are in fact specifying all files with any name, and any extension, i.e. all files on the given disk, to be deleted, copied, etc..

Example 1

> copy a:*.* b:

is a special way of commanding the computer to make a copy of all files on the disk in drive A and placing the copies on the disk in drive B. Notice that no filenames are specified for the copies, thus forcing the computer to give the copies the same names as the original filenames.

Example 2

> del a:*.*

is very effective and dangerous. It commands the computer to delete all files on the specified drive. If you type this command, you will be asked if you are sure about it. This is an automatic safety measure to help you to avoid making mistakes.

Example 3

del *.*

is likely to cause most users some problems sometime in their computer lives. Notice that the drive specification has been omitted. This is quite all right, but it forces the computer to assume that the appropriate drive is the current drive.

This is where the problem can arise. For example, the user may think he is going to delete all files on the disk in drive B, whereas the computer has other ideas as the current drive is really drive A. You can say bye-bye to all the important files on the disk in the drive A unless you've been careful enough to write-protect this disk.

Here's another example; let's say you've been using your word processor program to write some very important documents. You exit your word processor and decide to you want to erase all the files on a diskette in drive A since you don't need them any more. You type:

del *.*

What you meant to do was delete all the files on the A disk, but since you were logged onto drive C when you exited the word processor, what you've really done is delete all the files on the current directory of your hard disk. Then, unless you've got a skilled friend standing by with the proper program for un-erasing deleted files, be prepared for a tricky explanation telling your project leader why you will be late with your documents!

Fortunately, DOS will give you one last chance by asking you to confirm your intentions before going ahead with the deletion process.

One way of avoiding this is, especially when using the DEL command, by always specifying the drive letter even though DOS doesn't require it. YOU HAVE BEEN WARNED!

Exercise 1 - Filenames

Look at the following table and answer Y or N as to whether the given filenames are proper DOS filenames. The answers are on the next page.

Filename	Answer (Y or N)	Reason if N
PCPROD		
hello.1		
Newcastle.txt		
oFFer		
inv 01.doc		
file1+2.txt		
happy.doc		
OFF/093		
MYFILE.*		
446.doc		
1table.tab		
prog.exe		
file01.file		
DATE,01		
HEAVYDUTY		
TYPE"1".DOC		
fLoWers.dba		
XX123.wx		
byebye.doc		
middle001.sx		

Answers to exercise 1

Filename	Answer (Y or N)	Reason if N
PCPROD	Y	
hello.1	Y	
Newcastle.txt	N	Name too long (max 8+3)
oFFer	Y	
inv 01.doc	N	Space not allowed
file1+2.txt	N	+ not allowed
happy.doc	Y	
OFF/093	N	/ not allowed
MYFILE.*	N	* not allowed
446.doc	Y	
1table.tab	Y	
prog.exe	Y	
file01.file	N	Extension too long (max 3)
DATE,01	N	, not allowed
HEAVYDUTY	N	Name too long
TYPE"1".DOC	N	" not allowed
fLoWers.dba	Y	
XX123.wx	Y	
byebye.doc	Y	
middle001.sx	N	Name too long

Exercise 2 - The ? wildcard

Look at the following table and answer Y or N as to whether the filenames in the second column match those in the first column. The answers are on the next page.

Filename with ? wildcard	Matching filename	Answer (Y or N)
MYFILE.00?	MYFILE.001	
MYFILE.???	MYFILE.123	
FLOW?RS.DOC	FLOWERS.DOC	
P?.DOC	P11.DOC	
QQ.?	QQ	
ACC?.DAT	ACC8.DAT	
ACC?.DAT	ACC9.DAT	
ACC?.DAT	ACC10.DAT	
LOOK?.FIL	LOOK.FIL	
E?.TXT	ENGINE.TXT	

Answers to exercise 2

Filename with ? wildcard	*Matching filename*	*Answer (Y or N)*
MYFILE.00?	MYFILE.001	Y
MYFILE.???	MYFILE.123	Y
FLOW?RS.DOC	FLOWERS.DOC	Y
P?.DOC	P11.DOC	N
QQ.?	QQ	N
ACC?.DAT	ACC8.DAT	Y
ACC?.DAT	ACC9.DAT	Y
ACC?.DAT	ACC10.DAT	N
LOOK?.FIL	LOOK.FIL	N
E?.TXT	ENGINE.TXT	N

*Exercise 3 - The * wildcard*

Look at the following table and answer Y or N as to whether the filenames in the second column match those in the first column. The answers are given on the next page.

Filename with * wildcard	Matching filename	Answer (Y or N)
FILES.*	FILES01.DOC	
ACC*.*	ACC01.DAT	
.	MYFILE.DOC	
*.DOC	WATER	
E*.T*	EXTRA.TXT	
DE*.T*	DERBY.DOC	
Q*	QUICK.TXT	
F*.*	FIRE.DAT	
ROYAL.*	ROYAL1.ERM	
MA*.DAT	MAIL01.DAT	

Answers to exercise 3

Filename with * wildcard	Matching filename	Answer (Y or N)
FILES.*	FILES01.DOC	N
ACC*.*	ACC01.DAT	Y
.	MYFILE.DOC	Y
*.DOC	WATER	N
E*.T*	EXTRA.TXT	Y
DE*.T*	DERBY.DOC	N
Q*	QUICK.TXT	N
F*.*	FIRE.DAT	Y
ROYAL.*	ROYAL1.ERM	N
MA*.DAT	MAIL01.DAT	Y

Subdirectories and Pathnames

Why do all computers these days have hard disks? The answer is simple. Hard disks can store much larger volumes of information, compared with diskettes, and they work much faster.

The smallest of hard disks generally in use today is 40 Mb, and can store 40 million bytes, or characters, i.e. the equivalent of 20,000 pages of a book, and that is considered these days to be a very small hard disk! Hard disks which store up to 600 million bytes are not unusual, and larger ones are available.

With so much storage space available, a hard disk will often have several thousand different files on it. The secret of a hard disk is... well try guessing! How would you like it if every morning you went to your wardrobe to get some clothes, only to find thousands of different items of clothing lying in one big unsorted heap? Don't you have your shirts in one place, your socks in another etc.?

This chapter will not help you get dressed in the morning, but it does provide invaluable information for the hard disk owner. Some DOS commands and concepts will be introduced in this chapter, and there are many exercises in later chapters to put them into use.

Organising your hard disk

To be able to find a given file, amongst the hundreds of files you may have on your hard disk, some sort of organisation is needed. The answer is to divide the hard disk into different areas, which are called directories in computer language.

A hard disk divided into different directories, is a well structured system, just like any reasonably large company would be structured. You can build this structure to suit your own needs.

A hard disk always has one main directory, which is always called the *root directory*.

When you create new directories, these can be placed structurally directly under the root directory, or under any other existing directory. Directories which are positioned under another directory, are referred to as subdirectories. Consider this example:

> *First you create three special directories, one each for your word processor, spreadsheet, and database programs.*

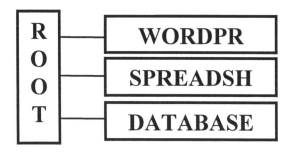

> *All files connected with your word processor would be stored in the word processor directory. Let's say that you use your word processor for writing letters, and that you have some main areas of writing, like company letters, private letters, information sheets, and other areas. You could then create subdirectories to your word processor directory, to store each type of letter in.*

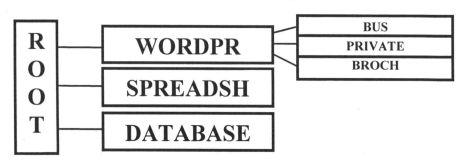

In this way, you can build up a hard disk structure to suit your own needs. All files can be placed in a relevant directory, making it much easier to find them when needed.

The overall structure you create is called a *directory tree*, and DOS actually has a command called TREE that will let you inspect the structure of your hard disk. If you are using Windows' File Manager, or the DOS Shell program, the directory structure will be shown automatically.

You can also build the same sort of structure on a diskette, but because the storage volume is so limited, it is not really practical to do so.

The current, or working directory

With a structure of directories on your hard disk, your computer needs to know which directory it should be working with. This is done automatically by DOS, by using a *current directory*, or *working directory*, which stays the same until you issue a command to change it. Thus DOS keeps track of the current directory in the same way that it keeps track of the current drive (A, B, C, etc.).

To show the user which directory is the current one, the system prompt can be extended to show the name of the current directory, for example:

```
C:\>
```
```
C:\WORDPROC>
```
```
C:\WORDPROC\PRIVATE>
```

All levels of the current directory are shown.

The symbol \

Looking at the examples above, you will see the backslash (\) symbol being used. This has two different meanings, depending on its position.

The \ symbol directly after the drive name (with its colon), signifies the root directory. When naming a directory, the computer always starts from the root directory and works down through the tree like structure of a hard disk. Thus the root directory symbol \ is always shown first. All other directories have their own specific name, the root directory has the name \.

When used further down in a structure, in what is called the *pathname*, the \ symbol is used to separate the names of the different directories and subdirectories from each other.

The pathname

In the example structure, there is a directory named PRIVATE. This is the actual name of that directory. PRIVATE is, however, a subdirectory of the WORDPROC directory, which is itself a subdirectory of the ROOT directory.

The pathname, gives the complete route that the computer will have to travel to find a given directory, starting from the drive name and root directory.

For this example, the actual directory name is PRIVATE, but its pathname is C:\WORDPROC\PRIVATE.

It is possible to have two or more directories with the same name, for example PRIVATE, but their pathnames will be different, e.g.:

> C:\WORDPROC\PRIVATE
> C:\DATABASE\PRIVATE

The PROMPT pg command

As mentioned, the extended system prompt showing the current directory and its pathname, can be used. This is just about a necessity for hard disk users. Unfortunately, however, it is not an automatic feature, and your computer has to be instructed to do this with a special DOS command. On the other hand, if your computer has been installed for you, it will probably be set up to automatically give this command every time you start it.

You will notice if you get the extended system prompt. If you don't, then the prompt will always be the plain C:> prompt, irrespective of the name of the current directory. In such a case, you should do the following:

- Check if ONLY the system prompt C:> is displayed on your screen (not C:\> ,for example).

- If necessary, type the following;

  prompt pg

- Press the **Enter** key.

The extended system prompt will thereafter be shown.

Software

Application programs, usually referred to as *software,* or just *programs*, are what enable your computer to perform so many different tasks. Without software, you couldn't do anything more than sit and look at your computer and maybe wonder why you didn't buy something more artistic or amusing!

There are literally thousands of programs available on the market allowing you to perform hundreds of different tasks in tens of different ways. The prices vary enormously from just a few pounds to over £1000. Most programs, however, fall into a few main categories as explained here.

Word processing

Word processing is by far the most common use for a computer. It allows you to type letters, reports, books, etc. Having typed in a text, you can print it out, save it and use it again, or change it. You can copy, delete and move blocks of text and use special features like **bold text** and underlining. The following picture is taken from Microsoft Word for Windows v6, a very advanced and capable word processor program.

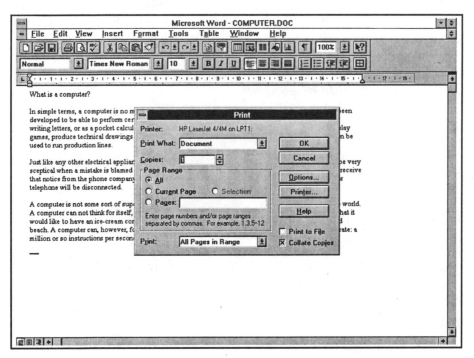

Some of the features you may be interested in are explained below.

Spelling checker

A spelling checker allows you to check for spelling mistakes. This course book has been checked with a spelling checker, but... if the word *field* is spelt *filed* by mistake, the spelling checker will not find the mistake because *filed* is a proper word. It will not find 'wrong words' only mis-spelt words.

Grammar checker

Some word processor packages now include a grammar checker, allowing you to look for grammatical errors. There are also some independent grammar checkers available if your word processor does not have this feature.

Thesaurus

A thesaurus will allow you to search for synonyms, useful for those times when a particular word is stuck on the tip of your tongue.

Mail merge and addressing envelopes

If you want to do maildrops, the mail merge feature will allow you to set up a main letter, a list of names and addresses and then automatically merge the two to print a series of individually addressed letters. Your word processor may also allow you to print addresses directly onto envelopes, or onto labels.

Indexing and table of contents

If you write longer documents, or manuals, you will find the ability to automatically produce contents tables and indexes most helpful. The table of contents for this course book took about 2 minutes to produce, automatically.

Spreadsheets

A spreadsheet program is like a glorious calculator. You can set up rows and columns of figures and use the program to perform all sorts of calculations. Having set up your spreadsheet model, you can then perform "What if?" analyses by testing different values and seeing what the result may be. What will happen to the cash flow if sales drop by 10%?

The following picture is from Microsoft Excel.

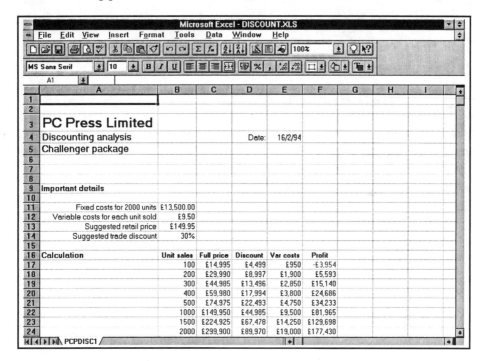

Charts and graphics

More advanced spreadsheet packages will allow you to create charts directly from your figures, and also pictures produced in other programs.

Databases

Database programs are used to store information. It could be names and addresses, product items, a collection of stamps or CD's. The main features of a database are that you can sort the data in different orders, search for individual records or groups of records, and produce reports. Databases can store text, numbers, dates and often pictures if advanced enough.

Relational database programs

A relational database program allows you to create several databases that share common information. This means that information need only be stored once and that the information can be accessed from different databases, saving a lot of storage space and time.

SQL

SQL stands for Standard Query Language and provides a standardised format for questioning a database. Many database programs are not SQL compatible, but some have add-on SQL modules.

Accounting programs

Accounting programs are, of course, used for accounts. They can be simple book-keeping programs or full-blooded order, stock and invoicing programs. Most accounting programs are modular, which means that you can buy a basic package and add on the modules you need

Graphics

Graphics programs are used to produce pictures and drawings. There are two types of picture as far as a computer is concerned. Pictures that are made up of dots are referred to as paint programs, and pictures made up of lines are referred to as drawing programs. In a paint program, a straight line is just a series of dots. In a drawing program, a straight line is stored as information such as the starting point and length and direction, so the program can draw the line. The picture below is from Windows Paintbrush.

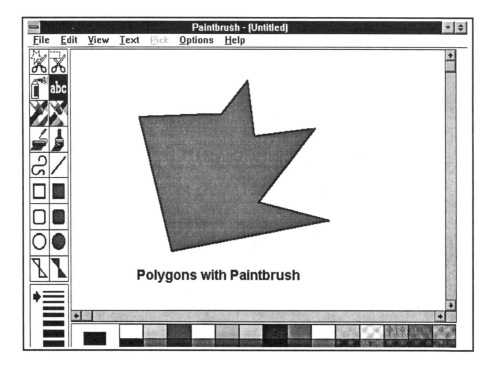

CAD

CAD, or Computer Aided Design, is a very advanced drawing program that allows you to produce very detailed and complicated drawings - and simple ones too! CAD is used for designing buildings, electronic circuit boards, cars, to name but a few examples.

Presentation packages

Business and presentation packages produce materials for overhead projectors, slides, etc. Typically they combine charts and diagrams with texts.

Desk top publishing

Desktop publishing is the art of producing printed matter - documents, books, brochures, etc., on a computer system. Texts and pictures can be combined to complete a final original that can be printed directly from the computer, and/or sent off to a print shop. The whole of this book was produced with a desk top publishing program.

The picture below shows Corel Ventura for Windows.

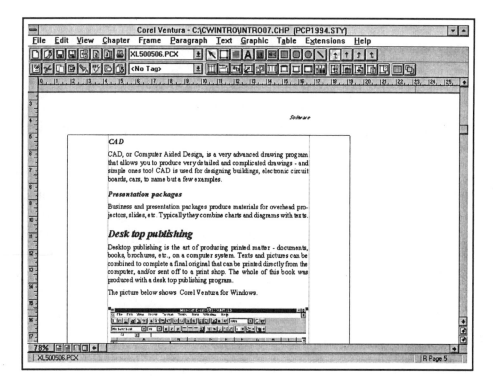

Communications

The whole idea of communications is to transfer data between two computers. For groups of computers within the same company, for example, this need is catered for by setting up networks (see next section). However, communications allows you to connect computers at any distance, even on the other side of the world.

The main reasons for computer communications are:

☺ Information retrieval, i.e. fetching information from any of the large information databases around the world.

☺ File transference, i.e. sending and receiving files of any type - documents, letters, accounts, drawings.

☺ Electronic mail, i.e. special systems for sending mail to other computer users.

The whole of chapter 22 is dedicated to communications.

Networks

Networks differ from general communications by connecting two or more computers, often tens or even a hundred, so that they can share common information and accessories. Thus, for example, somebody working on station X can save a text file on a central file server, and that same file can be picked up and edited by a user on station F.

Networks normally also have a mailing system for sending mail to all users connected to the network. The picture on the next page shows a message being created in Windows for Workgroups.

Generally networks tend to cause problems, and having an appointed network supervisor is a must. However, the problems caused appear to be outweighed by the advantages or else networks would have died out long ago.

Utilities

Utility programs help you in different ways to do small routine tasks. Some examples are:

- ⏏ Backing up and restoring files

- ⏏ Hard disk organisation and compression

- ⏏ File encryption

- ⏏ Recovery of corrupted files

- ⏏ Recovery after a hard disk crash

- ⏏ Virus finding and monitoring

Games

There is almost no need to mention that there are many many games of very differing standards and covering many many topics.

Specialised programs

Specialised programs can cater for almost any need. Route-finding, the Bible, Grammar checking, the night sky, satellite systems, the list is endless.

Shareware and Public Domain programs

Shareware is a concept where programs can be bought and tried for only a few pounds, and if you like the program you then send the suggested fee directly to the program author. Public Domain programs are similar, but there is no fee involved.

There are literally thousands of Shareware and Public Domain programs available covering an enormous range of topics. However, the quality of the program itself and its documentation vary a very great deal.

Getting Started

This chapter provides a gentle introduction to starting and using your computer.

Connecting all the cables

There are only a few connections to be made before you can use your computer. Even if your computer is ready to go, you may like to check the following connections.

⊛ Keyboard to system unit, with a round plug.

⊛ Monitor to system unit, with a 9 or 14 pin connector.

⊛ Monitor to power supply, either direct to a mains socket, or by a lead connected to the system unit. If the monitor is connected directly to the mains, you will need to turn it on and off independently from the system unit. If the monitor is connected to the system unit, it can be left turned on as turning the system unit on and off will then control the monitor power supply.

⊛ Printer to system unit (optional).

⊛ Mouse to system unit (optional).

⊛ System unit (and printer) to mains power supply.

The cables and connectors are designed so that you cannot plug them in wrongly!

Useful information before you start

Drive A

When starting a computer without a hard disk, you will need to put your DOS disk in drive A. If you have two drives, one on top of the other, the upper drive is usually drive A. If they are side by side, then the left hand drive is normally drive A.

If you only have one floppy disk drive, then your computer is able to pretend that you have two by switching the identity of the drive between A and B, as necessary. When you start your computer the drive will automatically be given the A identity.

Right side up

When putting a floppy disk into a drive, there are eight different ways of doing it, seven of which are wrong!

☺   The label on the disk should be on the top side and nearest to you.

☺   With both kinds of disks the write-protection notch should be on the left hand side.

If you put the disk in the wrong way, your computer will not be able to use it. A message will be shown on your screen that will say that the disk is not ready for use. If this happens, just take out the disk and put it back in the right way.

Starting the computer

As mentioned above, your monitor will either get its power from the system unit of the computer, or directly from an electrical outlet. In both cases, you will need to check that the power switch to the monitor is turned on.

•   Switch on your monitor.

If your monitor gets its power from the system unit, nothing will happen at this point.

•   If your computer is a floppy based system (i.e. no hard disk), insert your DOS, or system disk, in drive A, making sure it is the right way, and that you close the drive properly.

•   Switch on your computer.

What happens next depends on your computer and how it is set up, but the remainder of this section describes in general terms, what will happen.

Self-test

The computer will run a quick self-test to check that all of its parts are functioning properly. This will take as little a few seconds.

If any of the parts show a fault, a message will be displayed and the computer may not work. If this happens, switch everything off and start again. If you can't get the computer running after the second or third time, you will need the assistance of a more experienced user.

Load system files

You will notice some activity from your hard disk (or drive A if you are starting the computer from a diskette). The necessary system files are automatically loaded into your computer, where they are stored in RAM memory.

Many messages will also be displayed on your screen, but it is difficult to say just what they will be, as there are so many possibilities.

Date and Time

If you start your computer from a diskette you may be asked to confirm the current date and time. If so, you can confirm them by simply pressing the **Enter** key, or type in a new date or time.

Automatic program start

It may happen that your computer automatically starts a program, for example, Windows, DOS Shell or a menu system. However, it will not do so if it has not been especially programmed to do so.

The system prompt

Unless another program is automatically started, the system prompt, or DOS prompt, will be shown on your screen. This can differ from computer to computer, depending on whether you have a hard disk, and if your machine has been programmed to give a special system prompt. The most likely system prompts are shown below:

```
A:>
```

```
C:\>
```

If someone was a bit creative in setting up your computer, the system prompt might also tell you the time and/or the date. In any case, the system prompt is the computer's way of telling you that it is waiting for you to give it a command.

The cursor

The cursor is a blinking line (_), which shows you where the next thing you type in will be positioned on the screen. You will see the cursor together with the system prompt, or while running a program that requires an input from you. The form of the cursor may sometimes change into a solid box, and the rate at which it blinks may change.

Restarting your computer

It is possible to re-start (otherwise called boot, re-boot, or reset) your computer without switching anything off. If you do this, then everything currently stored in the computer's memory will disappear for good, so it can be a rather drastic step to take.

- Some computers will have a reset button, in which case you just press it.

- Some computers allow you to reset by turning a keyboard locking key, to a certain position.

- Another method is by depressing the following three keys at the same time: **Alt+Ctrl+Del**. Sometimes this method will not work, however, and you may have to switch everything off. If you are running Windows, you will need to read the message and press **Ctrl+Alt+Del** again.

- Reboot your computer now.

Switching off

There is nothing complicated about switching your computer off. Just make sure that you have saved any work you have done and then turn it off.

- Switch off your computer now.

Starting the computer from a diskette

When starting up your computer, it will automatically check to see if there is a diskette in drive A first, irrespective of whether you have a hard disk or not. If it finds one, it will try to start the computer using this diskette.

This means that you can start a computer from a diskette in drive A even if it has a hard disk. To be successful, however, the diskette must be a system diskette (or DOS diskette). It also means that if you try to start your computer with a diskette in drive A and that, for example, the diskette has some documents stored on it but is not a system diskette, the start-up will fail and you will get a Non-system diskette error message. In this case, you should simply remove the diskette from drive A and press any key (non-hard disk computers will also require a system diskette to be inserted).

The DIR command

* Start your computer again and wait for the system prompt to be displayed.

* If your computer automatically starts Windows or another program, exit this program to get the DOS prompt - you can exit Windows by pressing **Alt+F4**, or selecting **File**, **Exit**.

The first DOS command which you will learn about, is the DIR command. DIR is short for directory, and the command will give you a list of contents for a specified disk. DIR is an *internal DOS command*, which means that it is always available at the system prompt.

The general rule for DIR

The general rule for the DIR command, is as follows:

☝ Type **dir**, followed by a space, and then the name of the desired drive with its colon (:) after it. Press the **Enter** key.

☞ *When typing DOS commands such as **dir**, it doesn't matter if you use small or capital letters, or a mixture!*

What's on the exercise diskette?

Let's have a look at the contents of your exercise diskette supplied with this training course.

- Insert your exercise diskette in drive A.

- Type the following, be careful not to miss the space after the command word **dir**:

  dir a:

- Press the **Enter** key.

Your computer will now follow the instruction to list the contents of the disk in drive A. A list of files present will be displayed. It will look something like this:

```
Volume in drive A is PCINTRO
Volume Serial Number is 1377-0FE3
Directory of A:\

GO        EXE     27120 93-06-14    11.13
TEST      EXE     92800 93-06-14    11.14
DEMO            <DIR>       93-05-24     8.27
DEMO1     TXT        45 93-06-14    11.02
DEMO2     TXT        45 93-06-14    11.03
DEMO3     TXT        45 93-06-14    11.03
EX1       HAC        43 93-06-14    11.03
EX2       HAC        43 93-06-14    11.04
EXFILE1   DOC        47 93-06-14    11.04
EXFILE2   DOC        47 93-06-14    11.04
EXFILE3   DOC        47 93-06-14    11.04
FILE1     TXT        45 93-06-14    11.05
FILE2     TXT        45 93-06-14    11.05
FILE3     TXT        45 93-06-14    11.05
TEST      HLP       311 93-06-14    11.06
COMM      TXT     12184 93-06-14    11.08

16 file(s)       132912 bytes
                 580608 bytes free
```

Information on the size of the files, and the dates when they were created, is also shown, together with some general information about the disk.

The TYPE command

The TYPE command gives you a way of looking at the contents of a file. TYPE is an internal DOS command that is always available at the system prompt.

The general rule for TYPE

The TYPE command has two parts to it:

- ① The actual command word TYPE, followed by a blank space to separate it from the following file name.

- ② The source file, i.e. the name of the desired file, including the drive where it can be found.

- Insert your exercise diskette in drive A.

- Type the following:

  type a:file1.txt

- Press the **Enter** key.

The contents of the file will be displayed on your screen:

```
PC Training Courseware

This is FILE1.TXT
```

On completion, the system prompt will be shown again.

Screen dumps

This section assumes that you have a printer connected to your computer, if not, or if you have a PostScript laser printer, ignore the instructions.

A screen dump sends a copy of the text displayed on your screen to your printer. If there are graphic displays included in the text, they may or may not print.

To obtain a screen dump, do the following:

- Make sure that your printer is switched on and ready to run.

- Press the **Print Screen** (or **PrtSc**) key.

👆 *Some keyboards require you to press* **Shift+PrtSc**.

A copy of the screen display will be printed out on your printer. If you have a laser printer, then you may need to do a form feed to print the sheet out.

The DATE command

Your computer keeps track of the current date. However, you may wish to change the recorded date, perhaps it is wrong, or perhaps you have been advised to in order to fool a computer virus.

Proceed as follows:

- At the system prompt, type:

  date

- Press the **Enter** key.

The currently stored date will be displayed.

```
Current date is Sat 18/08/1994
Enter new date (dd-mm-yy):_
```

👆 *Some computers may have a different date format, e.g. yy-mm-dd*.

You have two choices. Either you confirm the displayed date, or you enter a different one. This date will be used when your computer records when files are saved, and by some programs to save you the trouble of entering the date manually.

To confirm the displayed date, do the following:

- Press the **Enter** key.

To enter your own date, do the following:

- Type in the desired date, for example:

  23-09-94

- Press the **Enter** key.

The TIME command

Your computer also keeps track of the current time. However, you may wish to change the recorded time.

Proceed as follows:

- At the system prompt, type:

  time

- Press the **Enter** key.

The currently stored time will be displayed.

```
Current time is 08:17:35:26
Enter correct time:_
```

You have the same two choices; either confirm the displayed time, or enter a different time.

To confirm the displayed time, do the following:

- Press the **Enter** key.

To enter a new time, do the following:

- Type in the desired time, for example:

  19:18

Note that it is sufficient to give only the hour and the minutes.

- Press the **Enter** key.

The PRINT command

In this final section, you will try out the PRINT command. This is a method of printing out a text file, other than using your word processing program. If you do not have a printer, or if you have a PostScript laser printer then skip the instructions.

- Make sure that your printer is switched on and ready to run.

- Insert your exercise diskette in drive A.

- Type the following, not missing the space after the command word.

  print a:file1.txt

- Press the **Enter** key.

The following message asking for the output device will appear - [PRN] means the printer:

```
Name of list device [PRN]:
```

- Press the **Enter** key.

The file will now be printed on your printer. If you have a laser printer, then you may need to do a form feed to print the sheet out.

Running programs

To run a program, you have to type the specific name of that program. Normally, you will also have to change to the correct drive first.

On your exercise diskette there are three programs called GO.EXE, TEST.EXE and PCCR.BAT that you can run.

☞ *You don't need to type .EXE, .COM or .BAT to start programs with these file extensions.*

Proceed as follows:

- Insert your exercise diskette in drive A.

- Type:

  a:

- Press the **Enter** key.

- Type:

  go

- Press the **Enter** key.

This simply shows a screen of text about the exercise diskette.

- Press **Esc** to exit.

Try the TEST.EXE program - this merely shows a text file called COMM.TXT on your screen. You can browse through the file using **PageDown**.

- Type:

  test

- Press the **Enter** key.

- When you are ready, press **Esc** to exit.

Finally, try the PCCR.BAT program.

- Type:

  pccr

- Press the **Enter** key.

- If you have time, try the program out - the instructions are available by selecting **Help**.

- When you are ready, exit the program.

Closing down

You have now completed your introductory tour.

- Switch off your computer, screen and printer.

A Little About DOS Shell

DOS has a so called shell program DOSSHELL that provides a window from which you can perform different DOS commands. Although this book teaches you the basic DOS commands without using DOSSHELL, you may already have seen it, or may wish to use it later on. This chapter, therefore, will give a brief introduction to DOSSHELL.

- Start your computer.

- Make sure you have the DOS prompt C:\> - exit any programs that are automatically started when you start your computer.

- Type:

  dosshell

- Press **Enter**.

☞ *If DOSSHELL doesn't start now, repeat the above but type*
c:\dos\dosshell instead.

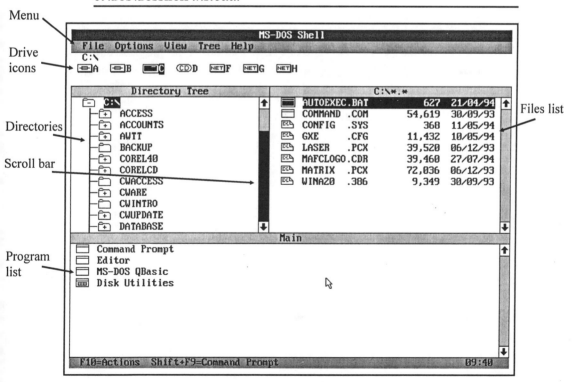

9-1

The DOS Shell window has 5 main areas:

Menu	Used to select the different options available.
Drive icons	Used to change the drive about which directory and file information is shown.
Directory tree	Shows the directories in the selected drive.
Files list	Show the files in the selected directory.
Programs list	A list of programs and program groups that can be used to start programs quickly.

Moving between the window areas

You can use the **Tab** key on the keyboard or click with the mouse to move between the different areas of the DOS Shell window.

- Press the **Tab** key 5 times, seeing how the highlight (probably blue) moves between the different window areas.

Selecting a drive

Now change the current drive - this is done by clicking on the desired drive icon with the mouse, or by pressing the **Ctrl** key together with the desired drive letter.

- Insert your exercise diskette in drive A.

- Use the mouse to click on the **A** drive icon, or just press **Ctrl+C**.

Note that both the Directory tree and the Files list are updated.

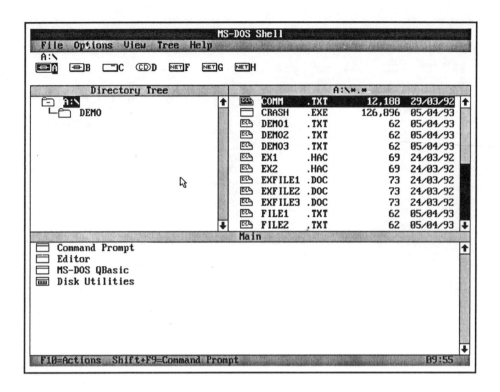

Using the menu

To open a menu you can use the mouse to click on the menu name at the top of the window, or press **F10** to activate the menu line, then choose the desired menu. You will now try one of each:

• Press **F10** to activate the menu.

Notice now that each of the menu titles has one letter underlined. This letter can be used to open that menu.

• Press **V** to open the **View** menu.

Again each of the options in the menu list has one letter underlined.

• Press **D** to select **Dual File Lists**.

The display is updated showing two sets of Directory trees and File lists.

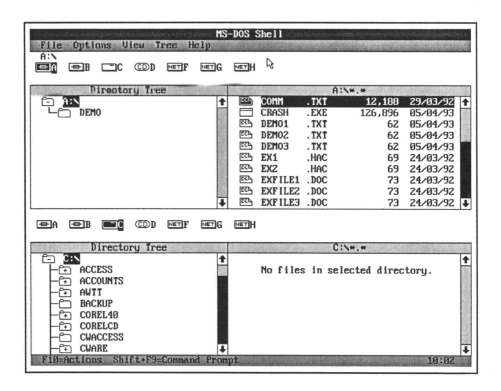

Now use the mouse to revert to only one set of file lists (if you don't have a mouse you will need to use the keyboard again - **F10**, **V**, **S**).

- Click on **View** in the menu line to open it.

- Click on the **Single File List** option.

The display reverts to showing just one file list. Notice that the Programs list is not shown.

- Click on **View** in the menu line to open it (or press **F10**).

- Click on the **Program/File Lists** option (or press **F**).

The Program list has now been restored.

Closing a menu without selecting an option

To close a menu without selecting an option, press **Esc**.

- Click on **View** in the menu line to open it (or press **F10**).

- Press **Esc** to close the menu.

Greyed menu options

Sometimes some menu options are not available at that particular moment. To indicate this, the menu option will be 'greyed out' and you cant select it.

- Click on **File** in the menu line to open it (or press **F10**).

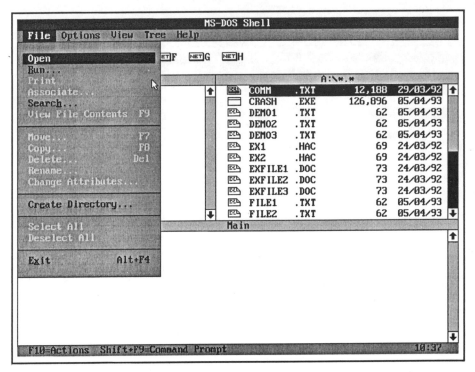

Notice that most of the options are greyed out and cannot be selected.

- Press **Esc** to close the menu.

Starting a program

You will now start the program PCCR.BAT supplied on your exercise diskette. To do this you have to select the filename PCCR.BAT in the list of files using the keyboard, or by doubleclicking on it with the mouse.

- Press the **Tab** key until the Files list is activated.

- Press the **ArrowDown** key until the file PCCR.BAT is highlighted.

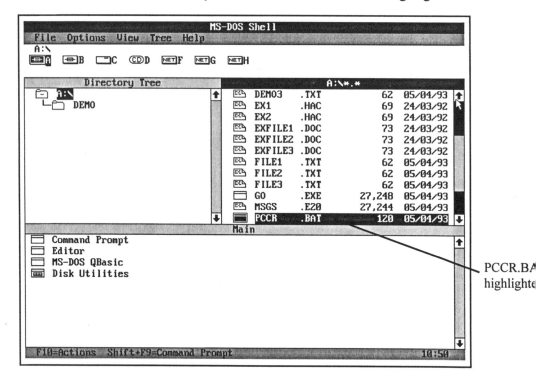

PCCR.BA highlighte

- Press **Enter** to start the program.

☞ *Using the mouse you can simply doubleclick on the desired filename, but you may have to use the scroll box to show the filename first.*

- Experiment with the program now if you wish to, all the instructions are available within the program.

- When you are ready, exit the program then press any key to return to the DOS Shell.

Viewing a file

The DOS Shell can be used to view files.

- In the files list, use the **ArrowUp** key to highlight the file COMM.TEXT (or click on it with the mouse).

- Open the **File** menu and select **View File Contents (F10, V)**.

The file is now displayed.

```
═══════════════════ MS-DOS Shell - COMM.TXT ═══════════════════
 Display  View  Help
┌ To view file's content use PgUp or PgDn or ↑ or ↓.            ┐
└                                                               ┘
COMMUNICATIONS CRASH COURSE by PETER HARRISON
=============================================

One of the most exciting areas in the world of computers is the possibility of
communicating with others. Just imagine being in touch, from your home or
office, with other users in New York, Rome, Tokyo or perhaps a remote farm in
the deepest forests of Sweden or any other isolated place!

If you're a beginner in communications, just inquisitive or one of those who
have accepted that communications probably is an exciting possibility "but
why the hell didn't it work for me..." then you should read this very basic
guide.

Why communicate?

People communicate either because it's fun or because it's necessary. Either  ▐
way, there are five main areas of communication:

1. Data transfer
            Data transfer involves sending data from one
            computer to another. Where the two computers are situated
            is not very important and the data can really be anything;
            a document or message, a set of financial reports, a picture,
            a program. Data transfers can be simple messages or, with the
            help of a specialised communications program, reports can be
 ◄─┘=PageDown  Esc=Cancel  F9=Hex/ASCII                       11:00
```

- Use **PageDown** to scroll the text downwards.

- When you are ready, press **Esc** to close the file.

Exiting DOS Shell

You have now finished your introductory tour of DOS Shell.

- Open the **File** menu and select **Exit** (**F10**, **X**).

FORMAT - Preparing Disks for Use

This chapter contains information about formatting disks and the exercises will take you through the necessary steps to format a diskette. If you feel you need more information about diskettes or hard disks, please check the chapter entitled **Data Storage**.

To be able to follow the exercises in this chapter, you will need at least one extra diskette, either completely new or a used diskette with no data stored on it that you wish to keep. If you have two diskette drives of different sizes, a diskette of each size will allow you to follow more of the exercises.

What is formatting?

Before you use a new diskette it needs to be prepared for use, this is formatting.

To give you an idea, think of a book. In order to print a book you need to know its size and how many pages there are. Then the actual story or information is printed onto the pages. The book will have a page of general details (i.e. the publisher, printer and date, etc.) and a table of contents at the beginning.

So what happens when you format a diskette? The overall storage capacity is decided (i.e. 720 kb, 1.44 Mb, etc.) and the diskette is divided into storage units rather like the pages of a book. These are called sectors and tracks. Your files can be copied onto the storage units just as text is printed onto the pages of a book. Formatting also reserves an area for the table of contents, called the root directory, and a couple of areas for its own use, called the boot sector and the FAT (file allocation table).

Fortunately, the storage units on a diskette can easily be wiped clean and used again. This would be equivalent to writing a book in pencil, rubbing it out, and writing something else!

Re-formatting

Diskettes can also be re-formatted and can be compared to shredding a book and recycling the paper ready for re-printing. Although diskettes aren't physically shredded, the files you have stored are lost.

How to format a diskette

To format a diskette you use the FORMAT command. The complicated part for the inexperienced user is deciding which parameters to use in order to let the computer know what sort of diskette you wish to format. If you are uncertain about what is meant by high capacity disk drives or high-density (HD) and double-density diskettes (DD), then you should now go back and read about these in the chapter entitled **Data Storage**.

Simple formatting rules

☺ You can only format 3.5" diskettes in 3.5" disk drives and 5.25" diskettes in 5.25" disk drives (surprised?).

☺ You cannot format a high density diskette in a disk drive that is not a high capacity drive. That is, you cannot format a 1.44 Mb 3.5" HD diskette in a standard 3.5" drive, and you cannot format a 1.2Mb 5.25" HD diskette in a standard 5.25" drive.

☺ If you have a high capacity drive, you can format both HD diskettes and DD diskettes. That is, if you have a high capacity 3.5" drive you can use it to format a 1.44 Mb 3.5" HD diskette or a 720 kb 3.5" DD diskette. If you have a high capacity 5.25" drive you can use it to format a 1.2 Mb 5.25" HD diskette or a 360 kb 5.25" DD diskette.

FORMAT switches

To format a diskette of any size or type the DOS command FORMAT is used. By giving the plain **format** command (e.g. **format a:**) DOS will attempt to format a diskette of the same type as the diskette drive. Thus, if you have a high-density 3.5" drive then DOS will attempt to format the diskette as a high-density 3.5" diskette (1.44 Mb). What if the diskette is not a high-density diskette? This will cause problems.

To overcome such problems, the FORMAT command can be appended with a number of so-called switches that result in unique commands for all combinations of diskettes and drives. The easiest way to present this information is in the form of a table, as follows:

| Drive type | Diskette to format | | | |
	5.25" (360 kb)	5.25" (1.2 Mb)	3.5" (720 kb)	3.5" (1.44 Mb)
5.25"	format a:			
5.25" HD	format a:/4	format a:		
3.5"			format a:	
3.5" HD			format a:/f:720	format a:

The shaded sections denote that it is not possible to format with that combination. Also all occurrences of a: can be replaced with b: if you wish to format a diskette in drive B instead.

From the table it is possible to find some rules, which are now presented together with a few other general points.

- If the drive and diskette to be formatted are of the same type, then it is enough to just type the format command together with the relevant drive letter, e.g. **format a:**.

- If the drive is a high-density drive and you wish to format a standard diskette, then you need to modify the format command, e.g.. **format a:/4** for 5.25" diskettes, **format b:/f:720** for 3.5" diskettes.

- If you try to format a high-density diskette in a standard disk drive, formatting will not be able to proceed.

- If you try to format a standard diskette in a high-density drive without modifying the format command, formatting will proceed until the diskette runs out of space. You will notice by the noise that the drive is struggling and it is best to cancel the process by pressing **Ctrl+C**, and then re-type the format command.

Formatting a system disk

It is possible to format a diskette as a system diskette doing so automatically adds the necessary system files onto the diskette. A system diskette can be used to start your computer (if your computer does not have a hard disk, you will already have a system diskette that you use to start it). Indeed, it is advisable to have a system diskette available in case your hard disk does not work one day when you switch on your computer. The system disk will at least allow you to get the computer started and to investigate what has happened.

⊕   To format a system diskette, just add /s to your format command, e.g.. **format a:/s** or e.g.. **format a:/4/s**.

Giving a diskette a volume name

It is also possible to give the diskette a special name called the volume. This can be up to 11 characters long.

⊕   To give the diskette a special volume name (up to 11 characters) just add /v to the format command, e.g.. **format a:/v** or **format a:/4/s/v**.

Formatting a hard disk

Before starting the exercises, it is worth pointing out that you can also format a hard disk by giving the command **format c:/s**, or **format d:**. If you do this, all data on your hard disk will be lost.

Formatting exercises

The remainder of this chapter is dedicated to formatting exercises.

With so many variations it would be pointless to try to ask any user to follow all the exercises. Therefore, the exercises are divided into a series of independent units and you should choose to follow those that suit your computer system and your needs.

Problems that may occur

When formatting a diskette several problems could arise. The most common are discussed here.

☺ Check that the diskette is in the right way round and the right way up.

☺ Check that your diskette is not write-protected.

☺ If you get a Bad track message the disk may be unusable and it is wisest to throw it away.

Other ways of formatting diskettes

Some programs will enable you to format diskettes by selecting the appropriate command from a menu. You may find it easier to use this method if you are already using such a program. These programs include:

Windows (use Disk, Format, in File Manager)
DOS shell
PC Tools and other utility programs

General points

To save repeating some things for every exercise, here are a few general points that apply throughout:

☺ Wherever the exercise refers to drive A and **format a:**, you may substitute this with drive B and **format b:**.

☺ If you choose to format an already formatted disk, you will be asked to confirm that you wish to go ahead with the format. Press **Y** to continue or **N** to cancel the format procedure.

List of exercises

The table below lists the exercises available.

Exercise no.		Format description
with hard disk	no hard disk	
1	7	1.44 Mb 3.5" HD disk in a high-capacity drive
2	8	720 kb 3.5" DD disk in a high-capacity drive
3	9	720 kb 3.5" DD disk in a standard drive
4	10	1.2 Mb 5.25" HD disk in a high-capacity drive
5	11	360 kb 5.25" DD disk in a high-capacity drive
6	12	360 kb 5.25" DD disk in a standard drive

☞ *CHOOSE ONLY THE EXERCISES APPROPRIATE TO YOUR SYSTEM. You need to know what sort of drive you have (high-density or not) and what sort of diskette you have (high-density or not). High-density 3.5" diskettes always have the letters HD printed on them.*

Systems with a hard disk

Most computers these days have a hard disk. Do relevant exercises chosen from 1 - 6.

Systems with no hard disk

Some computers may still have no hard disk, so exercises are provided where you need your DOS diskette with the FORMAT program on. Do relevant exercises chosen from 7 - 12.

Exercise 1

To format a 1.44 Mb 3.5" HD diskette in a high-capacity drive.

- Type:

   format a:

- Press the **Enter** key.

You will be prompted to insert the diskette to be formatted in the drive - do so.

- Insert the diskette in drive A.

- Press the **Enter** key.

The formatting will proceed and you will be asked if you wish to format another diskette.

- Press **N**.

To make a system diskette, use **format a:/s** instead.

Exercise 2

To format a 720 kb 3.5" DD diskette in a high-capacity drive.

- Type:

   format a:/f:720

- Press the **Enter** key.

You will be prompted to insert the diskette to be formatted in the drive - do so.

- Insert the diskette in drive A.

- Press the **Enter** key.

The formatting will proceed and you will be asked if you wish to format another diskette.

- Press **N**.

To create a system diskette, use **format a:/f:720/s** instead.

Exercise 3

To format a 720 kb 3.5" DD diskette in a standard drive.

- Type:

  format a:

- Press the **Enter** key.

You will be prompted to insert the diskette to be formatted in the drive - do so.

- Insert the diskette in drive A.

- Press the **Enter** key.

The formatting will proceed and you will be asked if you wish to format another diskette.

- Press **N**.

To create a system diskette, use **format a:/s** instead.

Exercise 4

To format a 1.2 Mb 5.25" HD diskette in a high-capacity drive.

- Type:

  format a:

- Press the **Enter** key.

You will be prompted to insert the diskette to be formatted in the drive - do so.

- Insert the diskette in drive A.

- Press the **Enter** key.

The formatting will proceed and you will be asked if you wish to format another diskette.

- Press **N**.

To create a system diskette, use **format a:/s** instead.

Exercise 5

To format a 360 kb 5.25" DD diskette in a high-capacity drive.

- Type:

  format a:/4

- Press the **Enter** key.

You will be prompted to insert the diskette to be formatted in the drive - do so.

- Insert the diskette in drive A.

- Press the **Enter** key.

The formatting will proceed and you will be asked if you wish to format another diskette.

- Press **N**.

To create a system diskette, use **format a:/4/s** instead.

Exercise 6

To format a 360 kb 5.25" DD diskette in a standard drive.

- Type:

  format a:

- Press the **Enter** key.

You will be prompted to insert the diskette to be formatted in the drive - do so.

- Insert the diskette in drive A.

- Press the **Enter** key.

The formatting will proceed and you will be asked if you wish to format another diskette.

- Press **N**.

To create a system diskette, use **format a:/s** instead.

Exercise 7

To format a 1.44 Mb 3.5" HD diskette in a high-capacity drive on a system with NO hard disk. To avoid errors, make sure that your DOS diskette is write-protected.

- Insert your DOS diskette in drive A.

- Type:

    a:

- Press the **Enter** key.

- Type:

    format a:

- Press the **Enter** key.

You will be prompted to insert the diskette to be formatted in the drive - do so.

- Insert the diskette in drive A.

- Press the **Enter** key.

The formatting will proceed and you will be asked if you wish to format another diskette.

- Press **N**.

To create a system diskette, use **format a:/s** instead.

Exercise 8

To format a 720 kb 3.5" DD diskette in a high-capacity drive on a system with NO hard disk. To avoid errors, make sure that your DOS diskette is write-protected.

- Insert your DOS diskette in drive A.

- Type:

    a:

- Press the **Enter** key.

- Type:

format a:/f:720

- Press the **Enter** key.

You will be prompted to insert the diskette to be formatted in the drive - do so.

- Insert the diskette in drive A.

- Press the **Enter** key.

The formatting will proceed and you will be asked if you wish to format another diskette.

- Press **N**.

To create a system diskette, use **format a:/f:720/s** instead.

Exercise 9

To format a 720 kb 3.5" DD diskette in a standard drive on a system with NO hard disk. To avoid errors, make sure that your DOS diskette is write-protected.

- Insert your DOS diskette in drive A.

- Type:

  a:

- Press the **Enter** key.

- Type:

  a:

- Press the **Enter** key.

- Type:

  format a:

- Press the **Enter** key.

You will be prompted to insert the diskette to be formatted in the drive - do so.

- Insert the diskette in drive A.

- Press the **Enter** key.

The formatting will proceed and you will be asked if you wish to format another diskette.

• Press **N**

To create a system diskette, use **format a:/s** instead.

Exercise 10

To format a 1.2 Mb 5.25" HD diskette in a high-capacity drive on a system with NO hard disk. To avoid errors, make sure that your DOS diskette is write-protected.

• Insert your DOS diskette in drive A.

• Type:

  a:

• Press the **Enter** key.

• Type:

  format a:

• Press the **Enter** key.

You will be prompted to insert the diskette to be formatted in the drive - do so.

• Insert the diskette in drive A.

• Press the **Enter** key.

The formatting will proceed and you will be asked if you wish to format another diskette.

• Press **N**.

To create a system diskette, use **format a:/s** instead.

Exercise 11

To format a 360 kb 5.25" DD diskette in a high-capacity drive on a system with NO hard disk. To avoid errors, make sure that your DOS diskette is write-protected.

- Insert your DOS diskette in drive A.

- Type:

  a:

- Press the **Enter** key.

- Type:

  format a:/4

- Press the **Enter** key.

You will be prompted to insert the diskette to be formatted in the drive - do so.

- Insert the diskette in drive A.

- Press the **Enter** key.

The formatting will proceed and you will be asked if you wish to format another diskette.

- Press **N**.

To create a system diskette, use **format a:/4/s** instead.

Exercise 12

To format a 360 kb 5.25" DD diskette in a standard drive on a system with NO hard disk. To avoid errors, make sure that your DOS diskette is write-protected.

- Insert your DOS diskette in drive A.

- Type:

  a:

- Press the **Enter** key.

- Type:

format a:

- Press the **Enter** key.

You will be prompted to insert the diskette to be formatted in the drive - do so.

- Insert the diskette in drive A.

- Press the **Enter** key.

The formatting will proceed and you will be asked if you wish to format another diskette.

- Press **N**.

To create a system diskette, use **format a:/s** instead.

MD - Making New Directories

MD is short for *Make Directory* and is the command used to create a subdirectory. This chapter explains the usage of the MD command with several exercises to follow. It assumes that you are conversant with subdirectories as explained in the earlier chapter entitled *Subdirectories and Pathnames*.

Subdirectories and diskettes

Please note that although it is not so common to work with subdirectories on diskettes, because of their limited storage capacity, it is quite possible to do so. Some of the exercises will get you to do this.

The root directory

Remember that the root directory (\) is automatically created whenever a diskette, or hard disk, is formatted.

General rule

The MD command has two parts to it:

⊛ The actual word **md**, followed by a blank space

⊛ The name of the subdirectory to be created, this can include a drive name and a full pathname

Some examples would be:

    md \database\company

    md test

    md a:\test

    md c:\pcprod\accounts

Considerations

☝ By only specifying the new subdirectory name you will create the new directory, as a subdirectory directly under the current directory.

☝ By specifying the complete pathname to an already existing directory, and then adding the new directory name, you can create a subdirectory anywhere in the directory structure.

☝ MD is an internal DOS command, i.e. it is always available at the DOS prompt.

☝ You are allowed to have more than one directory with the same name, but any given directory cannot have two subdirectories with the same name.

☝ Finally, remember that normal filename rules apply even for directory names, i.e. 1 to 8 characters.

Problems that may occur

There are really only a few problems that may occur:

☝ If you try to create a subdirectory that already exists, you will get an error message <u>Unable to create directory</u>.

☝ Your hard disk or diskette may be full so that you cannot create a subdirectory.

☝ You will not be able to create a subdirectory on a write-protected diskette.

The exercises

Exercise 1 will build up the following directory tree on your hard disk:

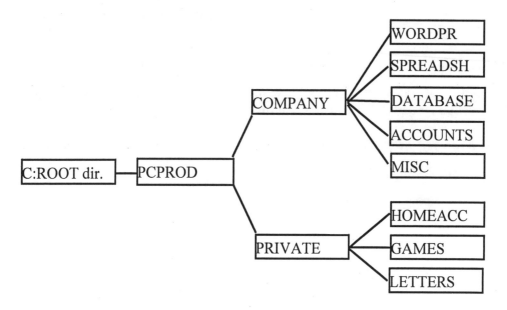

☞ *Subsequent chapters rely upon the existence of these subdirectories, so you should follow them in full.*

☞ *Don't worry about using up space on your hard disk, you will remove all the subdirectories at a later stage thus freeing the space again.*

☞ *If your computer does not have a hard disk it is possible to follow exercise 1 by replacing all occurrences of* **c:** *with* **a:***. You should then use a separate diskette for exercise 2.*

Exercise 2 will build up the following subdirectory tree on a diskette:

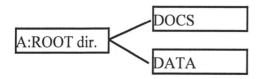

Exercise 1

Exercise 1 covers the following processes;

⊕ Making directories as subdirectories of the current or working directory

⊕ Making subdirectories anywhere in the directory tree

On a few occasions, you will use the CD command that is covered in the next chapter. Don't worry about this, just follow the instructions!

Making directories as subdirectories of the current directory

First of all, make sure that the root directory is the current directory:

● Type:

   **cd **

● Press the **Enter** key.

You can now make the main PCPROD subdirectory. Proceed as follows:

● Type:

   md pcprod

● Press the **Enter** key.

Now make the PCPROD subdirectory the current directory as follows:

● Type:

   cd pcprod

● Press the **Enter** key.

As PCPROD is now the current directory, you can easily make the COMPANY and PRIVATE subdirectories.

● Type:

   md company

● Press the **Enter** key.

- Type:

  md private

- Press the **Enter** key.

So far you have created the following directory tree:

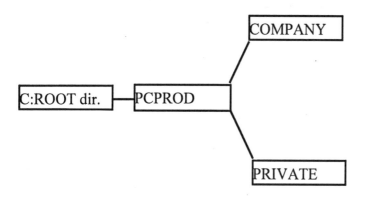

You can actually check this with the DOS command TREE, which will show you the subdirectories of the CURRENT directory.

- Type:

  tree

- Press the **Enter** key.

Now make the COMPANY subdirectory the current directory as follows:

- Type:

  cd company

- Press the **Enter** key.

As COMPANY is now the current directory, you can easily make the WORDPR, SPREADSH, DATABASE, ACCOUNTS and MISC subdirectories.

- Type:

    md wordpr

- Press the **Enter** key.

- Type:

    md spreadsh

- Press the **Enter** key.

- Type:

    md database

- Press the **Enter** key.

- Type:

    md accounts

- Press the **Enter** key.

- Type:

    md misc

- Press the **Enter** key.

You should now have created the following directory tree:

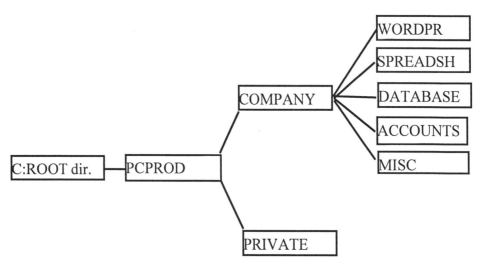

- Type:

   tree \pcprod

- Press the **Enter** key.

Making subdirectories anywhere in the directory tree

So far you have been creating subdirectories to the current directory only. This has involved using the CD command to change the current directory first.

You will now learn to create subdirectories anywhere in the directory tree, irrespective of what the current directory is. To do this you need to give the complete pathname of the subdirectory to be made.

Now create the following subdirectories:

☮ \PCPROD\PRIVATE\HOMEACC
   \PCPROD\PRIVATE\LETTERS
   \PCPROD\PRIVATE\GAMES
   \PCPROD\PRIVATE\MISC

Proceed as follows:

- Type:

   md \pcprod\private\homeacc

- Press the **Enter** key.

- Type:

   md \pcprod\private\letters

- Press the **Enter** key.

- Type:

   md \pcprod\private\games

- Press the **Enter** key.

- Type:

   md \pcprod\private\misc

- Press the **Enter** key.

You have now made the complete directory tree. Try **tree \pcprod** again.

Exercise 2

In this exercise you will create two subdirectories on a diskette. You will need a newly formatted diskette, or one that has some free space on it. Your exercise diskette will do if you have no other.

By adding drive name (e.g. **a:**) to the command before the subdirectory name, you can create a subdirectory on a drive that is not even the current drive.

- Insert a diskette in drive A.

- Type:

  md a:\docs

- Press the **Enter** key.

- Type:

  md a:\data

- Press the **Enter** key.

You have now created the following directory tree on the diskette:

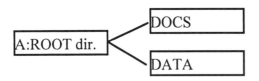

- Type:

  tree a:

- Press the **Enter** key.

☞ *If you used your exercise diskette, an extra subdirectory DEMO will also be shown.*

Summary

Remember that there are two ways of making a subdirectory:

- As a subdirectory of the current directory.

- As a subdirectory anywhere in the directory tree.

If you forget this, you will find (or not be able to find!) subdirectories in unexpected places.

Software packages and subdirectories

Most major software packages make and use their own directories. The knowledge you have gained here, however, will be most useful when you want to start storing documents and data files in an organised way.

CD - Changing Directories

CD is short for *Change Directory* and is the command used to change the current directory. Although you have already used this command in the previous chapter, this chapter explains the usage of the CD command in detail.

General rule

The CD command has two parts to it:

- The actual command word **cd**, followed by a blank space

- The name of the desired directory. This can include a full pathname

Some examples would be:

```
cd \
cd \wordproc\private
cd ..
```

Considerations

- By only specifying the desired subdirectory, you can move down one level in the directory tree, presuming that the subdirectory actually exists.

- By specifying the complete pathname of the desired subdirectory, you can change to any subdirectory in the directory tree.

- You can move up one level using the **cd ..** command. This will not work if the root directory (the top level of the directory tree) is already the current directory.

- CD is an internal DOS command, i.e. it is always available at the DOS prompt.

- You CANNOT change drives and directories in one go with a command such as **cd a:\docs**. Change drives first, then change directories.

⊕ DOS keeps track of the current directory for each drive. Thus if you swap to drive A and back to drive C, you will be returned to the same directory on drive C as when you left it.

Problems that may occur

The following are the most common problems:

⊕ If you try to change to a subdirectory that is not accessible, you will get an Invalid directory message. This may mean you have made a typing mistake, or that you should check the directory-subdirectory relationship to make sure you are not looking in the wrong place.

⊕ The extended system prompt (e.g. C:\PCPROD>) may not have been activated leaving the simple C:> system prompt irrespective of what the current directory actually is. This is only likely to happen for computers without a hard disk.

The solution is as follows:

⊕ At the system prompt, type:

prompt pg

⊕ Press the **Enter** key.

The exercises

As mentioned, there are several ways to move around a directory tree. The following table lists the exercises that cover each method and give an example command:

Ex. No.	Exercise description	Example
1	Automatically jump to the root directory	cd \
2	You can move down one level	cd games
3	You can move up one level using **cd ..**	cd..
4	Move directly to any subdirectory by giving the complete pathname	cd \pcprod\private
5	An exercise with a diskette	cd \docs

Exercise 1

Changing to the root directory.

Whatever the current directory is, you can always change to the root directory with one easy command.

- Type:

    c:

- Press the **Enter** key.

- Type:

    **cd **

- Press the **Enter** key.

Exercise 2

Moving down one subdirectory in the directory tree.

To quickly move down one level, you use the CD command together with the name of the desired subdirectory.

- Type:

  cd pcprod

- Press the **Enter** key.

Now use the DIR command to check the contents of the current directory.

- Type:

  dir

- Press the **Enter** key.

You should see a list of the subdirectories that are immediate subdirectories to PCPROD.

- Type:

  cd company

- Press the **Enter** key.

- Type:

  cd accounts

- Press the **Enter** key.

The following diagram shows how you have changed directories:

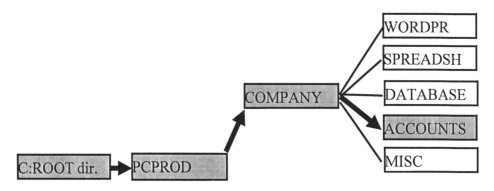

Exercise 3

Moving up one level in the directory tree.

You can quickly move up one level in the directory tree using the short command **cd ..** - i.e. cd with two full stops after it.

- Type:

    cd ..

- Press the **Enter** key.

You have now changed to the COMPANY directory.

- Type:

    cd ..

- Press the **Enter** key.

You have now changed back to the PCPROD directory.

Exercise 4

Changing to any directory in the directory tree.

You can change to any directory quite simply by including the full path-name of the directory.

- Type:

    cd \pcprod\private\games

- Press the **Enter** key.

- Type:

    cd \pcprod

- Press the **Enter** key.

- Type:

    cd \pcprod\company\database

- Press the **Enter** key.

Exercise 5

An example using diskettes.

- Insert the diskette that you used in the previous chapter into drive A.

- Type:

  a:

- Press the **Enter** key.

- Type:

  cd \docs

- Press the **Enter** key.

- Type:

  **cd **

- Press the **Enter** key.

Space or no space?

Some commands are acceptable both with and without a space after the **cd** part. For example, **cd..** is as good as **cd ..** and **cd** is as good as **cd **. However, whereas **cd pcprod** is OK, **cdpcprod** obviously isn't.

As a rule, it is ALWAYS acceptable to leave a space after the **cd** part of the command.

DIR - Listing Directories

DIR is short for *Directory* and is the command used to check a directory to see what files and subdirectories it contains. This chapter explains the usage of the DIR command. It assumes that you have read about wildcards, as explained in the chapter entitled *Filenames and Wildcards*, and also pathnames, as explained in the chapter entitled *Subdirectories and Pathnames*. If you are still uncertain about these two points, the practical exercises at the end of the chapter may well help to give you the understanding you need.

Directory listings

The DIR command is used to show a list of files contained in a directory. Any subdirectory to the directory you are listing will also be listed. From the list you will be able to see the names of the files and subdirectories which are present, and when they were created or last updated.

You can choose to see the complete list of a directory, or be selective by using wildcards.

It is also possible to print a copy of the contents of the directory directly on your printer. This is done in exercise 6.

The switches

/p   is used to show the list of files one page (i.e. screenful) at a time. This is very useful if a directory contains more than 20 files.

/w   is used to show the list in the wide format, i.e. four filenames per line with no information about the size and dates of the files.

General rule

- ④ The DIR command can be given on its own to list the contents of the current directory of the current drive.

- ④ The DIR command can be followed by a pathname to list the contents of any directory.

- ④ The DIR command can also be followed by a file mask, using wildcards to list groups of files, i.e. all files that have the extension DOC.

Some examples would be:

dir

dir /p

dir a:

dir a:/w

dir \database\company

dir *.doc

dir a:\test*.doc

Considerations

- ④ By only typing **dir**, you will get a directory listing of the current directory on the current drive.

- ④ By specifying the complete pathname to an already existing directory, you can check the contents of any directory.

- ④ DIR is an internal DOS command, i.e. its is always available at the DOS prompt.

The exercises

The table below describes the exercises that follow:

Exercise	Description
1	DIR current drive, current directory
2	DIR any drive, current directory
3	DIR any drive, current directory
4	DIR any drive, any directory
5	DIR with wildcards
6	DIR printing list on printer

The DIR command will also be used a lot in the next chapter.

Exercise 1

Listing the contents of the current directory of the current drive.

This exercise will help you check the contents of your exercise diskette, and of the root directory of your hard disk.

- Insert your exercise diskette in drive A.

- Type:

  a:

- Press the **Enter** key.

- If the root directory is not the current directory (i.e. if the prompt is something other than A:\>), then type:

  **cd **

- Press the **Enter** key.

- Type:

  dir

- Press the **Enter** key.

A list of the contents of the CURRENT directory of the diskette is now displayed.

- Type:

  dir /w

- Press the **Enter** key.

See the difference!

- Type:

  dir /p

- Press the **Enter** key.

- If necessary, press any key to see the next screenful of files.

Now check the root directory of your hard disk. If your computer does not have a hard disk you can use your system diskette instead - in which case you should ignore the next two instructions.

- Type:

  c:

- Press the **Enter** key.

- Type:

  **cd **

- Press the **Enter** key.

- Type:

  dir

- Press the **Enter** key.

A list of the contents of the root directory is now displayed.

- Type:

  dir /w

- Press the **Enter** key.

See the difference!

- Type:

  dir /p

- Press the **Enter** key.

- If necessary, press any key to see the next screenful of files.

Exercise 2

Listing the contents of the current directory of any drive.

To do this, simply type **dir** followed by the desired drive.

- Insert your exercise diskette in drive A.

- Type:

  dir a:

- Press the **Enter** key.

- Type:

  dir a:/w

- Press the **Enter** key.

- Type:

  dir c:

- Press the **Enter** key.

- Type:

  dir c:/w

- Press the **Enter** key.

- Insert any diskette in drive B.

- Type:

  dir b:

- Press the **Enter** key.

- Type:

  dir b:/w

- Press the **Enter** key.

Exercise 3

Listing the contents of any directory of the current drive.

To do this, simply type **dir** followed by the pathname for the desired directory.

First of all, make sure that C is the current drive.

- Type:

  c:

- Press the **Enter** key.

Now try a few directories:

- Type:

  dir \dos

- Press the **Enter** key.

- Type:

  dir \dos/w

- Press the **Enter** key.

- Type (this will not work if you do not have Windows):

  dir \windows

- Press the **Enter** key.

- Type:

  dir \windows/w

- Press the **Enter** key.

- Type:

  dir \pcprod\company

- Press the **Enter** key.

- Type:

  dir \pcprod\private\games

- Press the **Enter** key.

Exercise 4

Listing the contents of any directory of any drive.

To do this, simply type **dir** followed by the drive and the pathname for the desired directory.

Now try a few directories:

- Type:

  dir c:\dos/w

- Press the **Enter** key.

- Insert your exercise diskette in drive A.

- Type:

  dir a:\demo

- Press the **Enter** key.

- Type:

  dir c:\pcprod\company\database

- Press the **Enter** key.

Exercise 5

Using wildcards.

By using wildcards, you can choose to list a group of files rather than a complete directory list. This exercises combines the previous four, but adds a file mask.

- Insert your exercise diskette in drive A.

- Type:

  dir a:*.txt

- Press the **Enter** key.

- Type:

  dir a:\demo\demo*.*

- Press the **Enter** key.

- Type:

  dir c:\dos*.com

- Press the **Enter** key.

- Type:

  dir c:\dos*.com/w

- Press the **Enter** key.

- Type:

  dir c:\dos\c*.*

- Press the **Enter** key.

- Type:

  dir a:\f*.*

- Press the **Enter** key.

- Type:

  dir a:\f*.txt

- Press the **Enter** key.

Exercise 6

Listing the contents of a directory on your printer.

Sometimes it may be useful to have a printout of the directory list. To do this, simply add the parameter **>prn** to your **dir** command. Note, if you are using a laser printer, you may need to do a form feed to get the listing printed.

- Make sure your printer is on and ready to go.

- Insert your exercise diskette in drive A.

- Type:

  dir a: >prn

- Press the **Enter** key.

- Type:

  dir c:\dos/w >prn

- Press the **Enter** key.

- Type:

  dir a:\demo >prn

- Press the **Enter** key.

COPY - Copying Files

COPY the command used to copy files from one disk to another. This chapter explains the usage of the COPY command and assumes that you have read about wildcards, as explained in the chapter entitled **Filenames and Wildcards**, and also pathnames, as explained in the chapter entitled **Subdirectories and Pathnames**.

There are two main sections to this chapter. First of all, you will learn about the basic rule and do exercises using that rule. Then, in the second part, you will learn how to shorten the COPY command.

What is copying?

As the name suggests, if you have a file stored on a diskette or on your hard disk, you can make a copy of that file and store the copy on the same disk or on a different disk. Copying files is without doubt one of the most common activities, carried out by computer users. You can copy files one at a time, or in groups by using wildcards.

 Other methods of copying files are discussed at the end of this chapter, and also in later chapters.

The switches

/v   The COPY command has one useful switch that you can add, **/v**, or verify. This causes each file that is copied to be checked, by means of a checksum, to see if the copy process has worked correctly. The disadvantage of using this switch is the extra time taken for each file copied.

There are two other switches available, but these will not generally be used by a beginner. See your DOS manual for more information about the **/a** and **/b** switches.

General rule

The COPY command has three important parts:

- ☝ The word **copy**, followed by a blank space

- ☝ **From where** (the *source file*), i.e. the name of the file to be copied, this can include a full pathname

- ☝ **To where** (the *target file*), i.e. the filename to be given to the copy, including a pathname

Some examples would be:

> **copy file1.doc file2.doc**
>
> **copy a:myfile.doc c:\pcprod\newfile.doc**

Shortening the COPY command

It is possible to shorten the COPY command in many cases. This is done by leaving out information about the source and/or target files. If you leave out any information, whether intentionally or not, about which file to copy (*Source*), or where to copy it to (*Target*), DOS will assume default values on your behalf as follows:

- ☝ If you leave out the drive name in either part of the copy command, DOS will assume you mean the current drive.

- ☝ Similarly, if you leave out the directory in either part of the copy command, DOS will assume you mean the current directory.

- ☝ Finally, if you leave out the filename for the new copy, then it will be assumed that you wish to retain the same filename. Remember, however, that this will only work if you are copying a file to a different drive or directory as you cannot have two files with the same filename in the same directory.

So, assuming that C: is the current drive and \PCPROD is the current directory for C:, and that the root directory \ is the current directory for drive A, the following commands will have the same result:

> **copy c:\pcprod\myfile.doc a:\myfile.doc**

```
copy myfile.doc a:\myfile.doc

copy myfile.doc a:

copy \pcprod\myfile.doc a:\
```

Similarly, the following commands will all have the same result assuming that the current directories are \ on drive A and \PCPROD\COMPANY\WORDPR on drive C, and that C is the current drive:

```
copy a:\demo\demo1.txt c:\pcprod\wordpr\demo1.txt

copy a:\demo\demo1.txt \pcprod\wordpr\demo1.txt

copy a:\demo\demo1.txt demo1.txt

copy a:\demo\demo1.txt c:

copy a:\demo\demo1.txt c:\pcprod\wordpr
```

If you think that this all sounds very tricky, you may well be right. The exercises that follow will give you plenty of practise, but there is one way of always getting it right - that is by not shortening the COPY command at all!

The exercises

The table below describes the exercises that follow:

Exercise	Description
1	Copying files from the exercise disk to a hard disk
2	Copying files between directories on a hard disk
3	Copying files from a hard disk to a diskette
4	Copying files from one diskette to another diskette
5	Making an extra copy on the same drive and directory

All exercises use wildcards sometimes. If there is any exercise you cannot do, e.g. you have no hard disk, then just skip to the next exercise.

Exercise 1

Copying files from your exercise disk in drive A to the hard disk.

To do this, the source drive will always be drive A, and the target drive will always be your hard disk - drive C.

- Insert your exercise diskette in drive A.

Now make A the current drive.

- Type:

  a:

- Press the **Enter** key.

- Type:

  **cd **

- Press the **Enter** key.

Now copy a couple of files from drive A to the \PCPROD\PRIVATE\LET-TERS directory of drive C.

- Type:

  copy a:file1.txt c:\pcprod\private\letters

- Press the **Enter** key.

- Type:

  copy a:file2.txt c:\pcprod\private\letters

- Press the **Enter** key.

Notice that in both cases the filename of the copy was left out, thus making DOS use the same filename for the copy.

As A is the current drive, that information can also be left out of the source file part.

- Type:

  copy file1.txt c:\pcprod\private\letters

- Press the **Enter** key.

Similarly, we could make \PCPROD\PRIVATE\LETTERS the current directory of drive C, and use this fact to shorten the command.

- Type:

  c:

- Press the **Enter** key.

- Type:

  cd \pcprod\private\letters

- Press the **Enter** key.

- Type:

  copy a:file3.txt

- Press the **Enter** key.

Notice that as A is no longer the current drive, **a:** had to be added to the source file part once again. What about the target part? Nothing at all! Well, C is the current drive, thus can be omitted, \PCPROD\PRIVATE\LETTERS is the current directory and can also be omitted, and finally, the filename itself can be omitted leaving DOS to give the copy the same filename. Thus, all parts of the target file part were omitted!

To do the same thing again, but changing the filename this time, do as follows:

- Type:

  copy a:file3.txt file3xx.txt

- Press the **Enter** key.

Finally, use a wildcard to copy a group of files as follows:

- Type:

  copy a:exfile*.doc c:\pcprod\company\misc

- Press the **Enter** key.

- Type:

  copy a:\demo*.* c:\pcprod

- Press the **Enter** key.

- Type:

  copy a:ex*.hac c:\pcprod\private\homeacc

- Press the **Enter** key.

Can you work out what has been copied where? Try the following:

- Type:

  dir \pcprod

- Press the **Enter** key.

- Type:

  dir \pcprod\private\letters

- Press the **Enter** key.

- Type:

  dir \pcprod\company\misc

- Press the **Enter** key.

Exercise 2

Copying files between directories on your hard disk.

Let's assume that you have one hard disk, drive C, and wish to copy some files from one directory to another. C will always be source file drive and the target file drive, so assuming that you ensure C is the current drive first, you will always be able to omit **c:**.

- Type:

  c:

- Press the **Enter** key.

Now copy all the files from the \PCPROD directory to the \PCPROD\COMPANY\WORDPR directory.

- Type:

  copy \pcprod*.* \pcprod\company\wordpr

- Press the **Enter** key.

Notice that because both the source and target files included the correct directory paths, the copy procedure works irrespective of what the current directory is. Now do exactly the same copy command, but first having changed the current directory to \PCPROD.

- Type:

    cd \pcprod

- Press the **Enter** key.

- Type:

    copy *.* company\wordpr

- Press the **Enter** key.

See how both parts could be shortened by omitting **\pcprod** as \PCPROD is the current directory. Remember, if things get too complicated, then include the complete pathname for both source and target files!

Now do one final group copy.

- Type:

    copy \pcprod\company\misc*.* \pcprod\private\misc

- Press the **Enter** key.

Exercise 3

Copying files from your hard disk to a diskette in drive A.

To do this, the source drive will always be drive C, and the target drive will be drive A.

- Insert your exercise diskette in drive A.

Now make sure that C is the current drive and change the current directory to \PCPROD\PRIVATE\LETTERS.

- Type:

    c:

- Press the **Enter** key.

- Type:

    cd \pcprod\private\letters

- Press the **Enter** key.

Now copy a file from the hard disk to drive A.

- Type:

  copy file1.txt a:

- Press the **Enter** key.

Note that it was possible to leave out the drive and directory path of the source file.

Important concept

There is one important concept here...

Copying can destroy!!!

On your exercise diskette, there was a file named FILE1.TXT. You just copied a file from drive C with the same filename FILE1.TXT onto the diskette. As it is not permitted to have two files with the same filename in the same directory, the old file on the target drive is REPLACED by the new file you are copying. No warning is given. You have to be careful - if the older file on drive A had been an up-to-date important file, and the file that you just copied had been a useless file, you would just have lost the important file

On the other hand, if you are using a diskette to keep an extra copy of a file on your hard disk, you may wish to copy the latest version of that file onto the diskette each time using the same filename, overwriting older versions of the file.

Now copy another file from the hard disk to drive A, changing the name.

- Type:

  copy file1.txt a:file1xxx.txt

- Press the **Enter** key.

Finally, copy a group of files from a different directory onto drive A.

- Type:

  copy \pcprod*.* a:

- Press the **Enter** key.

Exercise 4

Copying files from one diskette to another.

In this case, whether you have one or two diskette drives, you can easily copy files between diskettes. If you do only have one diskette drive, DOS can use it as if it were two, by sometimes calling it drive A, and sometimes drive B. You will need two or more diskettes for this exercise.

- Insert your exercise diskette in drive A.

- Type:

  a:

- Press the **Enter** key.

- Type:

  copy file1.txt b:

- Press the **Enter** key.

DOS will start copying the file by reading its content. A message similar to the one below, will be shown:

```
Insert disk for drive B and
strike any key when ready
```

At this point, you should insert the diskette in drive B. If you only have one drive, this will mean removing the diskette in the drive and putting in the B diskette in the drive (you will have to swap back again soon).

- Insert the diskette in drive B.

- Press any key.

The copy process will eventually be completed.

Exercise 5

Making an extra copy on the same drive and directory.

This exercise really confirms something that has already been pointed out. You cannot have two files with the same name in the same directory. If you wish to keep two copies of the same file in the same directory, you will have to give the copy a different name.

- Insert your exercise diskette in drive A.

- Type:

  a:

- Press the **Enter** key.

- Type:

  copy file1.txt file1cop.txt

- Press the **Enter** key.

- Type:

  copy file1.txt file1.xxx

- Press the **Enter** key.

You now have three copies of the same file - FILE1.TXT, FILE1COP.TXT and FILE1.XXX.

- Type:

  c:

- Press the **Enter** key.

- Type:

  copy \pcprod\private\letters\file1.txt \pcprod\filex.txt

- Press the **Enter** key.

Other ways of copying files

There are other ways of copying files. Try DISKCOPY and XCOPY, as described in specific chapters towards the end of this course. For a complete back up, try BACKUP.

If you are very uncertain, there are special utility programs that will help you. PCTOOLS and NORTON UTILITIES are two such programs. These involve highlighting files that you wish to copy, and then highlighting drives and directories to which the file(s) should be copied.

WINDOWS and DOS SHELL also offer file copy procedures, but you will still need to have learnt the basics.

DEL - Deleting Files

The DEL command allows you to *delete* or *erase* files from your floppy and hard disks. You will, with time, be the proud owner of too many unwanted files and a clean-up will be necessary.

☻ DEL is an internal DOS command which means that it is always available at the DOS prompt.

General rule

The DEL command is made up of the following two parts:

☻ The command word **del**, followed by a blank space to separate it from the following file information.

☻ The name of the file to be deleted, which can include a full path-name.

Some examples would be:

del a:filex

This causes the computer to look for the file FILEX on the disk in drive A and delete it.

del b:fileq

This causes the computer to look for the file FILEQ on the disk in drive B and delete it.

Considerations

Before we go to the exercises, here's some additional information that most experienced users don't even know.

☞ *While the DEL command appears to wipe out the deleted file, in reality only the first character of the file's name is actually destroyed. This causes the file's name to disappear from your disk's directory, but all the data actually remains! I'm telling you this because at sometime you'll make a mistake and delete a file that shouldn't have been deleted. When this happens to you, it is often possible, with the right software, to recover a deleted file.*
When you find yourself in this position, the important thing is DON'T KEY IN ANY MORE COMMANDS TO THE COMPUTER, DON'T REBOOT IT, AND DON'T TURN IT OFF. If you can keep your head and remember this, you can then ask someone with greater computer knowledge and the proper software to help you save your file, and maybe your job!

del *.*

This special version of the command is likely to cause most users some problems sometime in their computer lives. Notice that the drive specification (A: or B:) has been omitted. This is quite all right, but it forces the computer to assume that the current drive and directory are the desired drive directory.

This is where the problem can arise. For example, the user may think he is going to delete all files on the disk in drive B, whereas the computer has other ideas as the current drive is really drive A. You can say bye-bye to all the important files on the disk in drive A unless you've been careful enough to write-protect this disk - or even worse if its drive C!

For instance, let's say you've been using your word processor program to write some very important documents. You exit your word processor and decide you want to erase all the files on a diskette in drive A since you don't need them any more. You type:

    del *.*

What you meant to do was delete all the files on the A disk, but since you were logged onto drive C when you exited the word processor, what you've really done is delete all the files on the current directory of your hard disk. Then, unless you've got a skilled friend standing by with the proper program for un-erasing deleted files, be prepared for a tricky explanation telling your project leader why you will be late with your documents!

One way of avoiding this, especially when using the DEL command, is by always specifying the drive letter even though DOS doesn't require it. YOU HAVE BEEN WARNED!

The exercises

The two exercises in this chapter will delete many of the files you copied onto your hard disk during the previous chapter. The remaining files will be deleted in the next chapter.

The table below describes the exercises that follow:

Exercise	Description
1	Deleting files from the current drive and directory
2	Deleting files from any drive and directory

Exercise 1

Deleting files from the current drive and directory.

The first exercise involves changing directories and then deleting files in the current directory. Proceed as follows:

- Type:

    c:

- Press the **Enter** key.

- Type:

    cd \pcprod\private\letters

- Press the **Enter** key.

Now check the files that are in this directory.

- Type:

    dir

- Press the **Enter** key.

Now delete the files FILE1.TXT and FILE2.TXT

- Type:

  del file1.txt

- Press the **Enter** key.

- Type:

  del file2.txt

- Press the **Enter** key.

Check the directory listing again to see that the files have been deleted.

- Type:

  dir

- Press the **Enter** key.

Of course, you could have deleted all the files in the current directory in one go using **del *.***, or **del f*.***. Do so:

- Type:

  del f*.*

- Press the **Enter** key.

The directory is now empty, although if you use **dir**, DOS will show that there are 2 files . [DIR] and .. [DIR] - these refer only to the directories not to any specific files.

Now change directories and delete all files as follows:

- Type:

  cd \pcprod\company\wordpr

- Press the **Enter** key.

- Type:

  del *.*

- Press the **Enter** key.

Because of the significance of this command, you are asked to confirm that you do want to delete all the files in the directory.

- Press the **Y** key.

- Press the **Enter** key.

Check that the directory is empty (except for the directories . [DIR] and ..
[DIR]):

- Type:

  dir

- Press the **Enter** key.

Exercise 2

Deleting files from any drive and directory.

You can also delete files on any drive and in any directory by simply
including a full pathname.

- Insert your exercise diskette in drive A.

Check the contents of the root directory of the diskette, for files starting
with F.

- Type:

  dir a:\f*.*

- Press the **Enter** key.

Now delete the files FILE1COP.TXT, FILE1XXX.TXT and FILE1.XXX
from the exercise diskette.

- Type:

  del a:\file1cop.txt

- Press the **Enter** key.

- Type:

  del a:\file1xxx.txt

- Press the **Enter** key.

- Type:

  del a:\file1.xxx

- Press the **Enter** key.

Check with the DIR command that these files have indeed been deleted
from the diskette.

Now delete all the files in the \PCPROD directory as follows:

- Type:

  del c:\pcprod*.*

- Press the **Enter** key.

Because of the significance of this command, you are asked to confirm that you do want to delete all the files in the directory.

- Press the **Y** key.

- Press the **Enter** key.

Finally, check that this directory is now empty of files:

- Type:

  dir \pcprod

- Press the **Enter** key.

☞ *The directory should actually be empty of files, but there will be other subdirectories present.*

RD - Removing Directories

RD is short for *Remove Directory* and is the command used to remove directories from your disk.

General rule

The RD command has two parts to it:

⊕ The actual command word **rd**, followed by a blank space.

⊕ The name of the subdirectory to be removed.

Some examples would be:

    rd \pcprod\company

    rd accounts

Considerations

⊕ By only specifying the actual directory name, you will delete the stated directory providing that it is a subdirectory to the current directory.

⊕ By specifying the complete pathname to an existing directory, you can delete a directory anywhere in the directory tree.

⊕ A directory can only be removed if it is empty, that is, it contains no files, and has no subdirectories of its own.

⊕ You cannot remove the current directory. If you wish to, you must first change directories and then remove the directory you changed from.

⊕ RD is an internal DOS command, i.e. it is always available at the DOS prompt.

Problems that may occur

The only problems you will have with this command are:

☺ The directory you wish to remove is not empty - it may contain a file or a subdirectory.

☺ If you only give the directory name without a full pathname, and the directory to be removed is not a subdirectory of the current directory, you will not be able to remove it.

The exercises

The following exercises will delete files and remove all of the directories that you have created during this course.

☺ *Exercise 1* will show you how to delete files and remove a subdirectory of the current directory.

☺ *Exercise 2* will show you how to remove a directory from anywhere in the directory tree.

☺ *Exercise 3* will show you how to delete file and remove directories from a diskette.

Exercise 1

Deleting all files and then removing a subdirectory to the current directory.

In this exercise you will delete all files in the directories HOMEACC, GAMES and MISC, removing the directories as you go. First change to the desired directory:

• Type:

  cd \pcprod\private\homeacc

• Press the **Enter** key.

Now delete all the files:

• Type:

  del *.*

• Press the **Enter** key.

- Press **Y** to confirm the file deletions.
- Press the **Enter** key.

Next check that the directory is empty of files:

- Type:

  dir

- Press the **Enter** key.

Assuming that the directory is empty you can move up one directory (remember that you cannot delete the current directory).

- Type:

  cd ..

- Press the **Enter** key.

Finally, delete the directory itself:

- Type:

  rd homeacc

- Press the **Enter** key.

Now repeat this with the other subdirectories of PRIVATE starting with the GAMES subdirectory, noting that some directories may already be empty.

- Type:

  cd games

- Press the **Enter** key.
- Type:

  del *.*

- Press the **Enter** key.
- Press **Y** to confirm the file deletions.
- Press the **Enter** key.

- Type:

  cd ..

- Press the **Enter** key.

- Type:

  rd games

- Press the **Enter** key.

Now clear and delete the MISC subdirectory.

- Type:

  cd misc

- Press the **Enter** key.

- Type:

  del *.*

- Press the **Enter** key.

- Press **Y** to confirm the file deletions.

- Press the **Enter** key.

- Type:

  cd ..

- Press the **Enter** key.

- Type:

  rd misc

- Press the **Enter** key.

Finally, clear and delete the LETTERS subdirectory.

- Type:

  cd letters

- Press the **Enter** key.

- Type:

  del *.*

- Press the **Enter** key.

- Press **Y** to confirm the file deletions.

- Press the **Enter** key.

- Type:

  cd ..

- Press the **Enter** key.

- Type:

  rd letters

- Press the **Enter** key.

All the subdirectories of PRIVATE have now been removed. Check this with the tree command:

- Type:

  tree

- Press the **Enter** key.

You should get the message <u>No subdirectories exist</u>.

Exercise 2

Removing any subdirectory.

This exercise assumes that the subdirectories to the COMPANY directory were cleared as described in the previous chapter. If not, you will need to clear them first.

- Type:

  cd \

- Press the **Enter** key.

- Type:

  rd \pcprod\company\wordpr

- Press the **Enter** key.

- Type:

  rd \pcprod\company\spreadsh

- Press the **Enter** key.

- Type:

  rd \pcprod\company\database

- Press the **Enter** key.

- Type:

  rd \pcprod\company\accounts

- Press the **Enter** key.

- Type:

  rd \pcprod\company\misc

- Press the **Enter** key.

Note that the directory is in fact not empty, and so the command is not performed. Proceed as follows:

- Type:

  del \pcprod\company\misc*.*

- Press the **Enter** key.

- Press **Y** to confirm the file deletions.

- Press the **Enter** key.

- Type:

  rd \pcprod\company\misc

- Press the **Enter** key.

The directory should now be removed successfully.

Now remove the two subdirectories of PCPROD, i.e. COMPANY and PRIVATE.

- Type:

  rd \pcprod\company

- Press the **Enter** key.

- Type:

  rd \pcprod\private

- Press the **Enter** key.

Finally, it is time to remove the PCPROD directory itself.

• Type:

   rd \pcprod

• Press the **Enter** key.

You have now cleared all the directories you once created.

Exercise 3

Removing directories from a diskette. If you try delete all files in a directory that is already empty, you will get a DOS error message <u>File not found</u>. This is nothing to worry about.

• Insert the diskette you have been using in drive A.

• Type:

   a:

• Press the **Enter** key.

• Type:

   del a:\docs*.*

• Press the **Enter** key.

• Press **Y** to confirm the file deletions.

• Press the **Enter** key.

• Type:

   rd a:\docs

• Press the **Enter** key.

• Type:

   del a:\data*.*

• Press the **Enter** key.

• Press **Y** to confirm the file deletions.

• Press the **Enter** key.

- Type:

  rd a:\data

- Press the **Enter** key.

The diskette is now cleared of the subdirectories you once created.

System Disks and Files

This chapter contains some general information about system disks and the system files COMMAND.COM, CONFIG.SYS and AUTOEXEC.BAT.

System disks

When you start your computer one of the first things it does is to search for and load two special system files and a file called COMMAND.COM which contains the basic commands used by DOS. Without these files the computer cannot start. The computer will then automatically search for two other files, CONFIG.SYS and AUTOEXEC.BAT.

Normally your computer will search for COMMAND.COM first on a diskette in drive A, and if there is no diskette in drive A it will then search for it in the root directory of your hard disk C. The fact that the computer first checks to see if there is a diskette in drive A allows you to use a diskette to start the computer even if you have a hard disk. This can be useful, or indeed necessary, if for example your hard disk breaks down, or you get a virus on your computer as you can then use a system disk to start it.

Creating a system disk

To create a system disk you use the FORMAT command together with the switch **/s**. This has been covered earlier in chapter 10. To follow the instructions below, you will need a new diskette, or a used diskette that does not contain any files you want - they will be wiped off!

- Make sure your computer is running and that you have the DOS prompt C:\.

- Insert the diskette in drive A.

- Type:

  format a:/s

- Press the **Enter** key.

After confirming your command the diskette will be formatted and the system files copied onto the diskette.

- Choose not to format another diskette.

Now check the directory of the diskette:

- Type:

  dir a:

- Press the **Enter** key.

The directory list should show that your diskette contains the file COM-MAND.COM. Don't forget to label it!

- Label the diskette as "SYSTEM DISK".

Testing your system disk

You will now try using your system diskette to start your computer.

- Make sure your system disk is in drive A.

- Re-start your computer (switch it off and on, or press the Reset button, or press **Ctrl+Alt+Delete**).

The computer will now start up from the diskette and will probably show less information than usual on your screen. It will also ask you to confirm the date and time, but will not start any other programs automatically.

- When prompted, press **Enter** to confirm the date.

- When prompted, press **Enter** to confirm the time.

Although your computer has been started from a diskette, you can still access your hard disk in the normal manner.

- Remove the system diskette from drive A.

- Re-start your computer again.

CONFIG.SYS

As mentioned earlier in this chapter, when starting up your computer will automatically search for and load the file CONFIG.SYS. This contains instructions for DOS on how to set up the available memory and other devices you may have installed. These days you will not normally need to alter this file yourself as most installation programs do it automatically. You can however check to see its contents.

- Make sure the DOS prompt C:\ is shown.

- Type:

    type config.sys

- Press the **Enter** key.

The contents of the file is listed - one example is shown below, from the first few lines you can see that this particular program runs Windows.

```
DEVICE=C:\WINDOWS\SMARTDRV.EXE /DOUBLE_BUFFER
DEVICE=C:\WINDOWS\HIMEM.SYS
DEVICE=C:\WINDOWS\EMM386.EXE NOEMS
BUFFERS=10,0
FILES=50
DOS=UMB
LASTDRIVE=Z
FCBS=4,0
DEVICE=C:\DOS\SETVER.EXE
DOS=HIGH
SHELL=C:\DOS\COMMAND.COM /P /E:1024
STACKS=9,256
COUNTRY=044,437,C:\DOS\COUNTRY.SYS
DEVICE=C:\SB16\DRV\SBCD.SYS /D:MSCD001 /P:220
DEVICE=C:\WINDOWS\IFSHLP.SYS
```

AUTOEXEC.BAT

Another file that your computer automatically searches for and loads is AUTOEXEC.BAT. It can be used to automatically run a program, or perform other commands, each time you start your computer.

List its contents as follows:

- Make sure the DOS prompt C:\ is shown.

- Type:

  type autoexec.bat

- Press the **Enter** key.

The contents of your AUTOEXEC.BAT will be listed. It is impossible to say what the file will contain on any individual computer as it is possible to set up this file to suit your personal needs. Here is an example of a typical AUTOEXEC.BAT file:

```
C:\WINDOWS\net start
LH /L:0;1,45488 /S C:\WINDOWS\SMARTDRV.EXE /X 2048 128
C:\DOS\DOSKEY /INSERT
SET SOUND=C:\SB16
SET BLASTER=A220 I10 D1 H7 P300 T6
C:\SB16\SBCONFIG.EXE /S
C:\SB16\SB16SET /M:220 /VOC:220 /CD:220 /MIDI:220 /LINE:220 /TREBLE:0
/MIC:220
LH /L:1,46576 C:\WINDOWS\MSCDEX.EXE /S /V /D:MSCD001 /M:15
PROMPT $P$G
PATH C:\WINDOWS;C:\WFWG;C:\DOS;c:\MOUSE;
LH /L:1,50144 c:\MOUSE\MOUSE
SET TEMP=C:\DOS
SET COMSPEC=C:\DOS\COMMAND.COM
LH /L:1,17856 C:\DOS\KEYB.COM UK,437,C:\DOS\KEYBOARD.SYS
SET MOUSE=C:\WINDOWS
C:\WINDOWS\MOUSE.COM
WIN
```

The first line shows that a network is being run on this computer, the last line gives the command to start Windows. In between there are various commands to run a sound card, a CD-ROM drive, a mouse and set up the keyboard for the UK. Don't worry about the details now as the contents of AUTOEXEC.BAT is generally set up and updated automatically as you install new programs and devices.

Backing Up Files

There is probably nothing more important than making copies, or back-ups, of your files. All the work you do at your computer can be lost forever if you don't make back-up copies. Files can be deleted and lost by mistake, your hard disk could break down, the computer could develop an electrical fault and start burning, you could be hit by a burglary and your computer stolen and sold off. At least if you have a copy of the files you have created, you will not have lost the work you have done.

Methods of backing up data

This chapter will concentrate on using the MSBACKUP program supplied with DOS v6, but there are other methods:

☺ If you regularly back up a large amount of files, you could invest in a tape streamer. This is a special tape unit for quickly storing large amounts of data on magnetic tape. Tapes can store from 40 Mb up to 650 Mb or more and the process can be automated - just imagine having back-ups done for you while you are at lunch!

☺ Optical and floptical drives can use special diskettes that can contain 30 Mb to 200 Mb. This is particularly useful for backing up large amounts of files.

☺ The DOS command BACKUP supplied with all versions of DOS - this is covered in Appendix B at the back of this course.

☺ The program MWBACKUP which is the Windows version of MSBACKUP covered in this chapter.

☺ Special programs also exist for backing-up files, such as PC TOOLS and NORTON UTILITIES.

What to back-up and how often?

Often it is not practical to back up your hard disk completely. Many hard disks these days are 200 Mb or more and a diskette can hold maybe 5 Mb using file compression, i.e. 40 diskettes at least! However, it is not really necessary to back up all files.

⊕ Programs can easily be installed again, presuming you have stored the original diskettes safely, and do not need to be backed up.

⊕ Accounts files and other files you work with (documents, spread-sheets, database files, etc.) should be backed up daily, or at the very least once a week. Most accounts programs include a back up facility and this can be used as a rule. Use one set of diskettes for each day of the week, or each week of the month, so that you always have several sets of back up disks.

⊕ AUTOEXEC.BAT and CONFIG.SYS should be backed up occasionally and specifically before you change them. These files contain a lot of settings for memory and other devices and can be hard to re-create.

Storing back ups

There is no point in making back up copies if you don't look after the copies! If you store them beside your computer and you are hit by a fire, the copies will be destroyed too! The following guidelines will help you:

⊕ Store back up disks in a safe place away from the computer, in a different room.

⊕ Important files should be stored in a fire-proof safe.

⊕ Really important files should have a separate back up copy to be stored in different premises altogether - e.g. one copy at work, one at home.

Using MSBACKUP

The remainder of this chapter shows you how to use the back up program MSBACKUP supplied with DOS from version 6. The program is quite advanced but the instructions that follow will take you through a simple example.

☞ *To follow the instructions in this chapter you will need an empty formatted disk for your back up. If you haven't got one just now you can still read and follow the instructions, but cancel the back up instead of starting it.*

☞ *You can run MSBACKUP directly from the DOS Shell program, but the instructions below assume that you will start the program from the DOS prompt.*

- Make sure the DOS prompt C:\> is displayed.

The program will be in the \DOS directory and you should be able to start it without changing directories, but to be on the safe side change directories first.

- Type:

  cd \dos

- Press the **Enter** key.

Now start the program.

- Type:

  msbackup

- Press the **Enter** key.

The main menu is displayed.

☞ *If it is the first time you use MSBACKUP you will get instructions about configuration and testing for compatibility. You must follow these instructions if they appear before proceeding.*

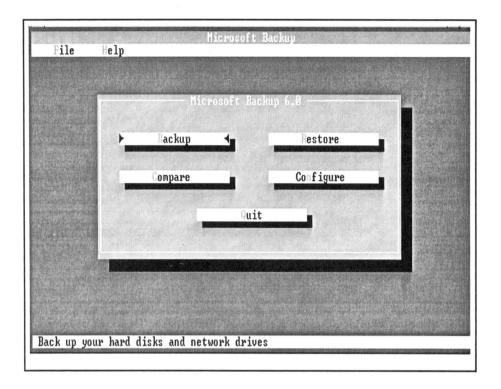

From the main menu you can choose to back up, restore, compare and configure.

- Select Backup by pressing **B** or by clicking on it.

The main Backup window is now displayed and you can choose which files to back up and where to store them. In our example, you will simply back up the CONFIG.SYS and AUTOEXEC.BAT files.

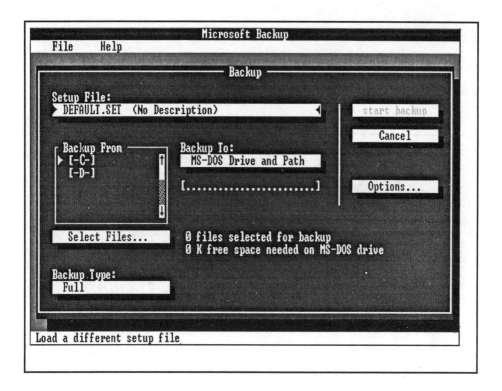

In this example you will choose to back up your CONFIG.SYS and AUTOEXEC.BAT files onto an empty formatted diskette.

Backup from and Backup to

You need to tell the computer which drive to back up from and which drive to back up to.

- In the Backup from box, select drive **[-C-]**.

- Select the Backup to entry to open a new dialog box.

- Select the drive and diskette type you will be using (e.g. **[-A-] Floppy 720 K 3.5**).

- Select **OK** to confirm your choice.

You are now returned to the previous window.

Selecting files for back up

Now you need to select which files you want to back up:

- Select the **Select Files** option.

The directories and files of the current drive are displayed.

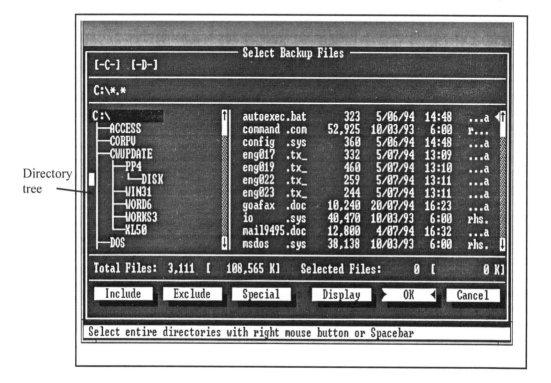

- In the Directory tree, make sure that the root directory C:\ is selected.

- Highlight the file autoexec.bat and select it by pressing the Spacebar (or just click on it using the right-hand mouse button) - the file
  will get a small tick to the left of its name.

- Repeat the above operation to select the file config.sys.

- Select **OK** to continue.

Starting the back up

You are now ready to do the back up.

- Select **Start Backup**.

- Follow the instructions you get on your screen - insert the empty formatted diskette as requested.

- When the back up is finished select **Cancel**.

- Select **Quit** to close MSBACKUP.

More information

For more information about MSBACKUP you can check your DOS
manual.

Memory Organisation and MEMMAKER

This chapter explains how the memory of your computer is organised and how to use the DOS program MEMMAKER which is supplied with DOS version 6.

Memory organisation

There are 5 types of memory that are talked about, although all 5 types are really internal divisions of the 1, 2, 4 or however many Mb of memory your computer has. The following picture shows the basic divisions:

```
┌─────────────────────────┐
│   Expanded/Extended      │
│        Memory            │
└─────────────────────────┘

┌─────────────────────────┐
│      High Memory         │
│         64 kb            │
└─────────────────────────┘

┌─────────────────────────┐
│     Upper Memory         │
│        384 kb            │
└─────────────────────────┘

┌─────────────────────────┐
│  Conventional Memory     │
│         640 kb           │
└─────────────────────────┘
```

Conventional memory is the first 640 kb of available memory. In days gone by computers had 640 kb or less and such a thing as memory problems didn't usually exist!

Upper memory is the next 384 kb of memory and is used by system hardware such as your screen. Unused parts of this memory are called *Upper Memory Blocks* (UMBs) and can be re-allocated for use by DOS.

Extended memory (XMS) is the extra memory above 1024 kb. These days machines will have 2, 4, 8, 16 or 32 Mb of memory. Extended memory requires a memory manager program like HIMEM.SYS to organise it. Windows and Windows programs require extended memory.

High memory (HMA) is the first 64 kb of extended memory and is used to install DOS into to leave more space free in the conventional memory.

Expanded memory (EMS) is required by some DOS programs and games when more memory than the conventional 640 kb is needed.

Using MEM to check the memory

DOS has a program called MEM that will display the current memory usage.

- Make sure the DOS prompt is displayed.

- Type:

  mem

- Press the **Enter** key.

The following shows the memory usage on a typical system with 16 Mb - the Upper memory (384 kb) is referred to as <u>Reserved</u>.

```
Memory Type        Total  =   Used  +   Free
----------------   -------   -------   -------
Conventional         640K       80K      560K
Upper                123K      123K        0K
Reserved             384K      384K        0K
Extended (XMS)    15,237K   14,213K    1,024K
----------------   -------   -------   -------
Total memory      16,384K   14,800K    1,584K

Total under 1 MB     763K      203K      560K

Largest executable program size        560K (573,376 bytes)
Largest free upper memory block          0K        (0 bytes)
MS-DOS is resident in the high memory area.
```

Using MEMMAKER

MEMMAKER is a program supplied with DOS v6 to help optimise your memory usage. You will need to know the following:

☺ Do any of your DOS based programs require expanded memory?

If you have DOS version 6 or later you can now try running MEMMAKER.

- Make sure that you have the DOS prompt C:\> - MEMMAKER cannot be run from inside Windows or the DOS shell.

- Make sure you don't have any other programs running.

- If your computer is usually connected to a network, make sure the network program is running.

- Type:

  memmaker

- Press the **Enter** key.

MEMMAKER presents an introductory text.

- Read through the text and then press **Enter** to continue (or **F3** if you want to quit).

Next you have to choose whether you want to run the Express setup or the Custom setup. At this stage it is recommended that you run the Express setup.

- Press the **Enter** key to continue with the Express setup.

Next you have to tell MEMMAKER if any of your programs require expanded memory. You may need to check the handbook for a particular program if you are unsure.

☞ *If you answer NO to the question about expanded memory, a program that actually requires expanded memory may not work next time you start it. You should run MEMMAKER again and choose YES instead.*

- If any programs require expanded memory press the **Spacebar** to change the answer to Yes.

- Press **Enter** to continue.

MEMMAKER now checks to see if Windows is installed on your system. It then displays a final message.

- Read the message.

- Make sure you do not have a diskette in drive A.

- Press **Enter** to continue.

Your computer will now re-start automatically and MEMMAKER will start up again with another message.

- Press **Enter** to continue.

Once again the computer will re-start.

- Check to see that you don't get any error messages as the computer starts up.

MEMMAKER will ask if everything seems to be working OK - do one of the following:

- **If everything seems OK**, press Enter to confirm it - MEMMAKER will update your CONFIG.SYS and AUTOEXEC.BAT files.

- **If you got any error messages or if something appears not to work OK**, press the Spacebar so that the answer No is shown, then press Enter - MEMMAKER will restore your original CONFIG.SYS and AUTOEXEC.BAT files.

MEMMAKER will now show what it has changed.

- Finish off by pressing **Enter**.

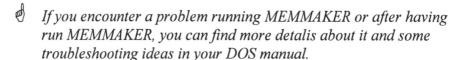 *If you encounter a problem running MEMMAKER or after having run MEMMAKER, you can find more detalis about it and some troubleshooting ideas in your DOS manual.*

Defragmenting Disks

When DOS saves your files on disk, it does not automatically save them as one long unit. Generally speaking, each file is divided into smaller units that fill one sector each on the hard disk. DOS will then fill in unused sectors anywhere on the disk so that one file may be spread out over a number of undetached sectors. From the beginning files will be saved in one long run, but as you save, overwrite and delete files more and more "holes" will appear on the disk and future files will be split - this is called fragmentation.

The net result of fragmentation is a slower hard disk. To read in a fragmented file the read/write head will have to be repositioned several times, so you will even hear the effects of loading and writing fragmented files.

The cure for fragmentation is disk compression or optimisation.

This chapter concentrates on using the DEFRAG program supplied with DOS version 6, but other similar third-party programs are available.

Using CHKDSK

Before you defragment a disk, you should check the disk for lost allocation units, these are small bits of files that no longer belong to a file, but can be converted to a file for inspection, use and/or eventual deletion.

- Close down all programs that are running.

- At the DOS prompt,type:

  chkdsk /f

☞ *If you want to check another disk you can type* **chkdsk d:** */f,* **chkdsk a:/f**, *etc.*

- Press **Enter**.

DOS now checks the current disk for lost allocation units. You will be given information on the disk, the number of files, etc.

If any lost allocation units are found you will see a message like this:

```
7 lost allocation units found in 3 chains,
Convert chains to files?
```

- If the above message is shown, press **Y**.

Using DEFRAG

You can now use DEFRAG to defragment the disk.

☞ *If a full defragmentation of your hard disk is required, and you have a large hard disk, the operation may take an hour or so, but you can leave the computer to get on with it itself. You may want to return to this chapter at a later date when you can then leave your computer running.*

- At the DOS prompt, type:

  defrag

- Press **Enter**.

DEFRAG will now do some checks before presenting its main display.

- First select the drive you wish to defragment - use **ArrowUp** and **ArrowDown** then press **Enter**.

DEFRAG will now read and analyse the disk.

☺ If you want more information about the current settings, or want to change the DEFRAG options select **Configure**.

For now, just start the defragmenting process:

- To begin defragmenting, press **Enter**.
- ☺ DEFRAG can be halted at any time by pressing **Esc**.
- Quit the program when it has finished.

Undeleting Files

When you delete a file, it is often possible to get it back again because, in effect, DOS only deletes the filename from the list of files on the disk. Not all files can be recovered, but if you do delete a file and then realise you wanted it, there is a good chance of success. If, however, you have carried on working and saved other files, the chances of success will have diminished.

In this chapter you will learn how to undelete a deleted file using the DOS program UNDELETE.

The 3 levels of UNDELETE

UNDELETE can be used in different ways as set out in the table below.

Delete Sentry	Provides the highest level of protection and requires small amounts of memory and disk space. It works by creating a hidden directory for storing deleted files.
Delete Tracker	Provides the next highest level of protection and requires small amounts of memory and disk space. It works by creating a special file that keeps track of the whereabouts of files.
Standard	Provides the lowest level of protection but requires no memory or disk space. You will be able to recover deleted files as long as DOS hasn't used the disk space to save another file over the top of it.

This course will show you how to use the Standard level. For more information on the other 2 levels you should consult your DOS manual.

Using UNDELETE

To use undelete you will first delete a file from your exercise diskette.

- Insert your exercise diskette in drive A.

UNDELETE can be used from Windows and the DOS Shell, but the instructions below are for use direct from the DOS prompt.

- At the DOS prompt type:

  del a:\demo1.txt

- Press **Enter**.

You have now deleted a file, so check it's gone:

- Type:

  dir a:

- Press **Enter**.

You should see that DEMO1.TXT is no longer in the list.

DOS has removed the first letter from the filename and it is no longer in the directory, but the file is still on the disk - so try and recover it!

- At the DOS prompt, type:

  undelete a:

- Press **Enter**.

UNDELETE now checks drive A for deleted files.

```
UNDELETE - A delete protection facility
Copyright (C) 1987-1993 Central Point Software, Inc.
All rights reserved.

Directory: A:\
File Specifications: *.*

    Delete Sentry control file not found.

    Deletion-tracking file not found.

    MS-DOS directory contains    1 deleted files.
    Of those,    1 files may be recovered.

Using the MS-DOS directory method.
        ?EMO1     TXT       62  5/04/93  9:35   ...A  Undelete (Y/N)?
```

It finds the deleted DEMO1.TXT file. Note how the first letter of the filename is missing.

- Press **Y** to undelete the file.

```
Please type the first character for ?EMO1    .TXT:
```

You are now asked to supply the first letter of the file.

- Type:

  d

The file is now recovered successfully, but check it is there again:

- Type:

  dir a:

- Press **Enter**.

You should see DEMO1.TXT in the list again.

Multiple files

Now try deleting and recovering all the files starting with F.

- At the DOS prompt type:

  del a:\f*.*

- Press **Enter**.

- Type:

  undelete a:

- Press **Enter**.

UNDELETE now checks drive A for deleted files and will ask you about them one at a time.

- For each file it finds, press **Y** to undelete it and then type the first letter of the filename (**f**).

You should now have successfully undeleted 3 files.

Viruses and Anti Virus Programs

Most computer users these days will have heard about PC viruses. Friday 13th has become more than a day for superstitions, it has become a day of worry for many users. Newspaper headlines and news broadcasts across the industrial world have spread fear amongst new and experienced computer people. The threat that computer viruses pose is becoming a regular topic in computer magazines.

What is a virus?

Basically a computer virus is a small computer program that manages to copy itself onto your computer - onto a floppy or hard disk. Think of them as weeds in your vegetable patch - they turn up without asking, and if you don't pull them out they will gradually take over the entire patch.

Some weeds are in fact quite attractive, but most of them are simply a nuisance. The same is true of computer viruses, a few are light-hearted or even humorous, the majority are, however, designed to damage the data you have stored on floppy or hard disks. That is why they are dangerous. In the worst-case scenario your computer could have a complete breakdown and you could loose all the information stored on your hard disk and on one or more of your floppy disks. If you don't want Fu Manchu or the Dark Avenger striking you down with a digital potato blight, then read on!

Here is a brief summary of some of the terms used in connection with computer viruses:

Virus	A small program that can copy itself "into" other programs. Viruses affect other existing programs and are dependent on them as they do not exist as complete programs themselves.
Time bomb	A small program section (normally destructive) that is activated when certain pre-defined conditions are met, e.g. a specific date and/or time, a specified period after being installed, a pre-defined keyboard sequence or a specified number of times a program is run.
Trojan horse	This is a program which will perform a specific normal task, just as any other program does, but also contains a hidden and undesirable part.
Bacteria or worms	Stand-alone programs, unlike viruses which 'attach' themselves to other programs, that create copies of themselves on the same computer and on other computers, thus decreasing available memory and 'choking' the computer.

Am I at risk?

Yes.

If you own a computer, or are responsible for one, for example at work, then you are at risk. If a virus strikes, then you may lose some vital information, and loose time by having to deal with the situation.

If you are an occasional user using somebody else's computer, then the risk is limited to the effect that you may loose some of your important work, apart from the possible embarrassment of having to tell the owner that his computer really ought to see a doctor.

If you are a nervous or reserved computer beginner, then you may well suffer psychologically as you realise that you have to face up to a very awkward situation with a total lack of confidence. Read on!

Catching viruses

"Catching viruses" should perhaps be re-phrased as "Getting caught by viruses" as no-one actually goes out looking for the things. The strange thing is that some users tend to be hypersensitive and a mere hiccup from their computer is construed as a true sign of a virus closing in for the kill, and "..wait till I get my hands on...?". Yes, who is the guilty one?

Seriously, many hitches, system hang-ups, computers going down, etc., depend on things other than viruses. Wrongly given commands, programs that do not work properly, variations in the power supply and memory resident programs can all cause problems that can be misconstrued as a virus.

Viruses move from one computer to another via floppy disks and communications. If you are given a floppy disk it could contain a virus that automatically copies itself onto your hard disk when you use the diskette. Having an infested diskette or hard disk could mean that the virus copies itself onto each diskette that you use, and can possibly be passed on to someone else. Thus viruses have a nasty habit of spreading, without anyone knowing anything about it.

If you accept a diskette from a friend or work mate, and use that diskette in your computer, then you put yourself at risk, although each time you do so the risk is very very small.

If you connect your computer to others, in a network or with the help of a communications program, then you also put yourself at risk. Again each time you do so the risk is very very small. BBS (Bulletin Board Systems) that have untested programs on offer are well-known virus transmitters.

.COM and .EXE files are hit

A virus works by "adding" its own program code to an existing program file - .COM or .EXE file, data files are not affected. For example your word processor that was 92 200 bytes in size could suddenly grow to 92 965 bytes in size - a true sign that it has been hit by a virus program.

Some viruses will affect important system files such as the COMMAND.COM file. Another type of virus affects the boot sector of diskettes, which is where vital information about the contents of the diskette is held.

Where do viruses come from?

Viruses are small computer programs. They are constructed by able programmers with a lot of time on their hands. Writing an effective virus program that doesn't give itself away is a time consuming process.

Some people see viruses as some sort of mischievous sport, good for a laugh. However, you cannot hide the fact that viruses constitute sabotage, a desire to inflict damage to other peoples' computers, programs and data.

Viruses have been traced from USA, UK, West Germany, Israel, Iceland, Bulgaria, India, Pakistan and many other countries.

Recognising viruses

Many computer users mistakenly think that they have been hit by a virus. If you have read about the example viruses, you will have some idea as to the kind of thing that can happen. If something strange happens to your computer you really need to keep your head and try and think "Have I done something wrong here?". The picture is complicated by the fact that there are bugs (mistakes) in some programs on sale that could cause odd things to happen. However, these are usually limited to a certain function of a program not working properly, or that the computer simply hangs.

For example, if sometimes when starting your computer it hangs, i.e. locks itself, several times before getting going, then this may be a particular hardware failure. If on the other hand it does so and at the same time gives off five beeps every now and again, then you should begin to ask yourself if it is a virus at large.

It can be very difficult trying to trace a virus. One virus called *Fumble* will hit anyone typing at faster speeds, i.e. a secretary. Calling in a techie to try and fix the bug will probably not reveal anything because he/she types to slowly to activate the virus. Some viruses are inspired mischievous sabotage!

If you have an original program diskette that you bought, check the size of the .COM and .EXE program files on the original diskette against the file sizes on your hard disk (be sure that the original diskettes are write-protected before doing so!). If any of the files have grown, then you should suspect a virus.

Preventive measures

There are some measures that you can take to protect yourself against viruses. A single PC is easier to protect than a system of computers connected together in a network.

- ☻ Get an Anti Virus program, or use the one supplied with DOS version 6 as instructed later in this chapter.

- ☻ Check your hard disk(s) for viruses.

- ☻ Check every diskette that you put into your computer.

- ☻ When you know your system is clean, prepare a system diskette (format a:/s) and write protect it. You then have a 'clean' diskette to start up your computer should you be hit by a virus.

- ☻ Always write-protect your original program diskettes before installing programs on your computer. Write-protection works as a virus preventive too. Write-protect other important diskettes that are not going to be written to.

As viruses often affect the important system file called COMMAND.COM, you should make a copy of this file on your hard disk or system diskette. Then compare the original COMMAND.COM file with the copy each time you start your computer. There is a special DOS command for doing this and you can put it in your AUTOEXEC.BAT file or type in the command each time you start your computer. When you start your computer you will then be notified if the two files are not the same, i.e. the COMMAND.COM file has mysteriously been changed. The steps are as follows:

- ☻ Make a copy of your COMMAND.COM file, calling it COMM.COM.

Now add the following command to your AUTOEXEC.BAT file:

fc command.com comm.cm

Note: Some DOS versions use **comp** instead of **fc**.

Now, each time you start your computer, it will check to see if the COMMAND.COM file matches the COMM.COM file, which it will not do if it has been attacked by a virus.

Anti-virus programs

Several programs that reveal the presence of viruses can be found on the market. They cannot help when a virus has already struck and your hard disk has been erased, but they can help you by warning you when a virus installs itself and in some cases even remove the virus or prevent it installing itself.

Using MSAV

MSAV is an anti virus program supplied with DOS version 6 or later. It has a Windows version called MWAV. The instructions that follow will show you how to use MSAV.

- At the DOS prompt, type:

  mwav

- Press **Enter**.

The Microsoft Anti-Virus program is started.

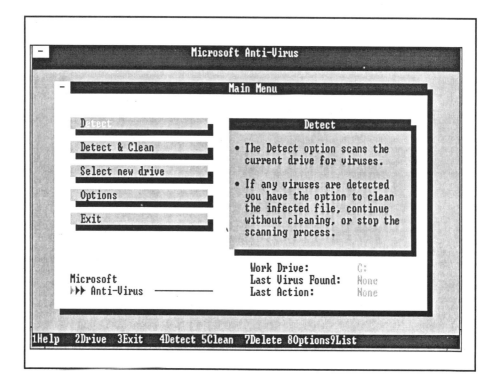

You can choose to **Detect** or **Detect and Clean**. Clean will attempt to remove viruses from your disk. The Work Drive is probably drive C:, if not you change it. Some options are also available - check your DOS manual for more information.

Checking your exercise diskette

As an exercise, you will now check your exercise diskette.

- Insert your exercise diskette in drive A.

- Select the **Select new drive** option.

A list of available drives is now shown along the top of the screen display.

- Select drive A.

- Select **Detect** to start the detection.

MSAV will now check the memory and then the diskette, looking for viruses. Hopefully there will not be a virus on the diskette. If there is, that doesn't mean it has come from the diskette, it could be on your computer and have transferred itself to the diskette already.

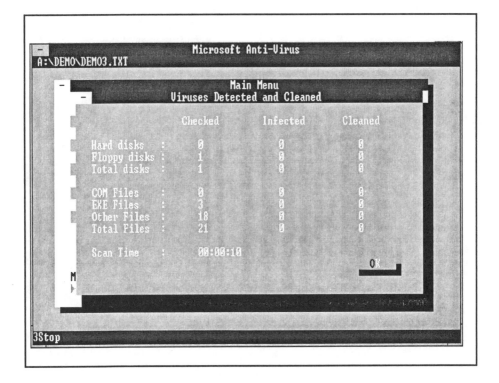

- Select **OK** to close the results.

- Select **Exit** to quit the program - you may also need to select **OK** to confirm the settings.

Do this now!

If you haven't already created a 'clean' system disk, you should do so now.

- Run the MSAV program to check the memory and hard disk is free from viruses.

- Create a system disk (format a:/s) and write protect it.

- Label the diskette "VIRUS FREE SYSTEM DISK" and store it in a safe place.

You can then use the system disk to start your computer if you are hit by a virus.

How Your Computer Works

This chapter is designed for people who would like to know a little more about how a computer works. The language used is non-technical so that anyone who has gotten this far in the book will be able to understand its contents.

The heart of a computer

Your heart beats about 70 times each minute. This varies from person to person, but we are all dependent on heart beats to send oxygen enriched blood through our body. A computer has no blood, but it does have a heart-like component. A clock inside the computer sends out pulses at regular intervals. Each pulse triggers the execution of an instruction which then flows within the computer from one part to another. Thus the computer is dependent upon the pulses of its clock, just as we're dependent upon the pulses of our heart.

The clock inside a computer sends out several million pulses per second. This differs from computer model to computer model. PCs and XT's have slower rates, AT's, 386, 486 and Pentium machines have faster ones.

You may have heard or read such terms as

    25 MHz processor
    40 MHz processor

This term measures the rate at which the clock is set to permit the processor (see next section) to work, in pulses per second. *25 MHz* is 25 million pulses per second.

The brains of a computer

A human brain is a very complex organ, capable of processing millions of electrical impulses coming from our five sense in a split second. A PC also has a sort of brain, which controls everything going on within a computer, at clock rates which currently range from 4 million to 25 million instructions per second. The computer's name is the *processor*.

Processors for IBM PCs and clones are manufactured by Intel Corporation and are given names such as the *8088* (used in plain PC and XT machines), *80286* (used in AT's or 286 machines), 80386 (used in the 386 machines) and 80486 (used in 486 machines).

What happens when you start your computer?

When you switch on your computer, it may take several seconds before it is ready to use. This does not happen because your machine is hung over or has morning sickness. No, for a healthy computer, the clock comes instantly up to its several million pulses per second and the processor feverishly sets about executing its instructions.

What happens is that the computer starts off with a kind of morning gymnastics routine, checking to see that all parts of its body are ready for the day's work. It automatically runs a *TEST program* to check that the keyboard, monitor and other parts are functioning properly.

Next, the computer will automatically load into its memory some system information, called *BIOS*, and then the internal DOS commands. BIOS stands for Basic Input Output System, and DOS stands for Disk Operating System.

DOS, as you probably know by this time, is a basic set of commands to help you access your disks. When you give a DOS command like COPY, DOS will call on the assistance of BIOS, to perform the copy process.

The final stage of the computer's warm-up is to look for any file information that it is pre-programmed to look for. This information is given in two special files, CONFIG.SYS and AUTOEXEC.BAT. Neither is necessary, but both are very common. You can inspect these files by using TYPE to print their contents on the screen (if they exist on your system disk - on a hard disk they will almost certainly exist).

When all of this is done, the system prompt will be shown along with the cursor. The computer is then ready to run the AUTOEXEC.BAT file. This file has the capability to automatically start another program, initiate a *menu system* which makes the computer easier for novices to use, or to change the way the system prompt or the cursor looks. Thus if your AUTOEXEC.BAT file has been programmed to put you right into the data entry mode of your database manager, or to display a menu with program names on your monitor, you may never see the system prompt.

What happens when you press a key?

When you press a key, a code number for the key pressed is automatically generated. That code number is placed in the keyboard buffer which is a kind of waiting room for keyboard code numbers.

Your computer checks at regular intervals -- many times a second -- to see if any code number is waiting to be picked up from the keyboard buffer. If one is, the code number is instantly moved to the computer's processor and assessed. The key stroke is then usually sent to the monitor so that you see what key you have pressed.

Please understand that all this happens in a flash. In fact your computer spends most of its time waiting for you to press a key!

Character representation

The computer does not work with keys and numbers, but only with electricity and voltage levels. Computer engineers define that a *high voltage* of about 5 volts is equivalent to 1, and a *low voltage* of around 0 volts is equivalent to 0. The 1's and 0's are then gathered into their own code, called *binary*, to represent numbers and letters. It is these binary codes which in turn build commands and other information.

Take the letter A, for example. This has been given the decimal code number 65, which translated to 1's and 0's in binary becomes 01000001 . Thus, if we have 8 electrical wires in which the voltage levels can be made either 0 or 5, we can represent that letter A by setting the voltages in the second and eighth wires to 5, and setting the others to 0.

In this way, it is easy to understand that a computer is only a simple electrical appliance. It deals only with electricity. When you press the A key, an A doesn't appear anywhere in the computer. The manufacturers have only printed an A on the key to make it easier for you. Pressing that key generates a series of electrical voltages. These are then processed within the computer, which in turn generates other voltages which cause your monitor to display the letter A again, by lighting up the necessary dots, or pixels, on your screen.

All this happens very, very quickly. If your computer's clock could only generate one pulse per second, instead of several million, it would take several minutes to show the letter A on the screen after you had pressed the A key.

Bits and bytes

Each single 1 or 0 is called a bit, i.e. it is a bit of a complete unit of information. A complete information unit is a group of 8 bits, and is called a byte.

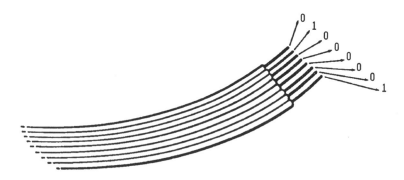

Each single bit, within a byte, can take the value 1 or 0. Each letter, number, or graphics character, has its own unique bit combination. The letter A is represented by 01000001, the number 7 by 00111001.

When we talk about the size of a computer's memory, we mean how many bytes, or characters, it is capable of storing. One kilobyte (1 kb) is the equivalent of 1024 bytes, so a computer with 640 kb memory can store 1024x640=655,360 bytes, or characters.

How is information stored?

You can think of a computer's memory as a large cupboard divided into thousands of pigeon holes. One byte of information can be stored in each pigeon hole. This means that to store the word FRANCE, 6 pigeon holes would be occupied, one for each letter of the word.

A computer with 640 kb memory, will have 655.360 pigeon holes in its cupboard. It keeps track of what's where, by numbering each hole from 0 to 655.360. When a character is to be stored in memory, it is given a numbered address, and stored accordingly.

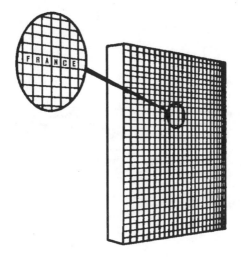

What happens when you run a program?

Most of the time you use your computer you will be running programs. When you start a program, a copy of the program is fetched from the relevant disk, and stored in the computer's memory. The original program information remains on the disk, your computer works only with the information it's copied into its memory.

During the running of the program, different parts of the memory will be used to store information used in that program. The computer automatically keeps track of where it places relevant information.

Your keyboard inputs will be processed, and instructions carried out, as defined in the program. The computer could not do anything without these program instructions.

What does a computer look like inside?

If you take the lid off your computer, which is not dangerous to either you or the computer so long as the power cable is disconnected, you will see a lot of green circuit boards, full of small black chips.

Each chip has its own tasks to perform. Some are memory chips. Others help to process keyboard inputs and the output to the monitor. The largest chip is most often the processor, the computer's brain.

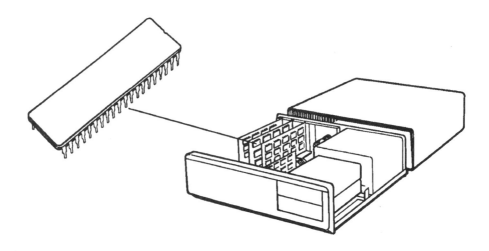

Every chip contains from a few, up to several hundred thousand transistors. During manufacture 95 per cent of all chips are thrown away; only a few work properly.

Other small components you can see are, capacitors, diodes, resistors and transistors.

Communications Crash Course

One of the most exciting areas in the world of computers is the possibility of communicating with others. Just imagine being in touch, from your home or office, with other users in New York, Rome, Tokyo or perhaps a remote farm in the deepest forests of Sweden or any other isolated place!

If you're a beginner in communications, just inquisitive or one of those who have accepted that communications probably is an exciting possibility "but why the hell didn't it work for me..." then you should read this very basic guide.

Why communicate?

People communicate either because it's fun or because it's necessary. Either way, there are five main areas of communication:

1. Data transfer

Data transfer involves sending data from one computer to another. Where the two computers are situated is not very important and the data can really be anything; a document or message, a set of financial reports, a picture, a program. Data transfers can be simple messages or, with the help of a specialised communications program, reports can be sent to hundreds of specified destinations at specified times. Computer programs can also be sent from one place to another.

2. Information retrieval

Around the world are many information services that provide databases through which you can access information and data on just about anything and everything. You can keep up to date with Wall Street using data provided by Dow Jones, check the times of flights to Seattle, or scan travel news, books, entertainments, press releases, scientific reports - to name just a few areas. A warning - searching for information can be expensive - so if you intend to do a lot of searching find out the costs first, and get instructions that will help you access information efficiently.

3. Control of a remote computer

Together with a specially designed program it is possible to sit by one computer and control another computer. You can for example use a computer at home to work with your office computer or a computer consultant could help you correct a problem on your computer without having to leave his/her office.

4. BBS - Bulletin Board Systems

A BBS is a sort of local communications centre to which several (often hundreds) users call to exchange messages, ideas and programs. Many software houses now have their own BBS acting as a support centre for their products.

5. Direct contact with other users

You can call another person and be in direct contact with them thus having an interactive communications session. You could for example exchange ideas and transmit files, and there are even on-line computer dating services!

What do I need?

Basically you need a communications program, a modem, a serial port on your computer and a telephone line.

Modem - What's that?

Modem is short for Modulator/demodulator. None the wiser? Well, a telephone line is best suited for a human voice and not for transmission of the sort of data your computer likes to send. A modem, which is connected between your computer and the telephone line, converts (modulates) the computer's data signals to more human-like tone signals, which can then be transmitted over the line. Another modem at the other end will receive the call and re-convert (demodulate) it to data signals which the receiving computer can understand.

A modem can either be a stand-alone unit connected to your computer's serial port and to a telephone line, or an add-in card which is mounted inside the computer.

The most important feature for a modem is it's transmission speed. This is measured in Baud or bps (bits per second) which are explained further on in this chapter. A higher Baud rate means a faster transmission and a lower telephone bill, but it also means a more expensive modem. It will be a question of measuring up your needs against your means.

Serial port

A serial port is a special sort of connector through which your computer can send data to the outside world, which might happen to be for example a modem or a serial printer.

If you have an external modem, i.e. stand-alone modem, then it will also have a serial port which has to be connected to a serial port on your computer.

Most computers have one, or two, serial ports, but it is possible that you will need to buy an extra serial port if, for example, you are using the present one(s) for a serial mouse and/or a serial printer, or some other computer add-on.

A serial port can have 9 or 25 pins. It's easy to check the back of your computer to see if you have a free serial port, but don't mix a 25 pin serial port with a 25 pin parallel port. You will have to buy the right sort of cable to connect the modem to your computer. When buying the cable it's important to state that your serial port has 9 or 25 pins and that it is for a modem because there are other sorts of serial cables designed for other uses.

What's next?

Assuming that you've correctly installed your modem, and installed and started your communications program (according to the manual supplied with the program!!!) everything can still go wrong! There are a lot of settings which must be right if you are not going to get a lot of garbled rubbish, or even get nothing at all happening when you try to communicate.

Some of the most important aspects of communications are explained in the following sections.

Protocol

The word *protocol* may sound more difficult than it is. A protocol is merely the collective name given to a set of rules which when followed will enable computers to communicate.

Synchronous and asynchronous transmission

Synchronous and asynchronous transmission relates to the "rhythm" to which data is transferred.

Synchronous transmission implies that data is transferred at a steady rate. Both the transmitting and receiving computers are synchronised at the start of a transfer session and the data is sent at a regular rate. If you feel your pulse (assuming it is regular) you can imagine that data is transmitted at each beat. For a computer, the beats are of course much much faster - even for those of you who have a high pulse!

Asynchronous transmission implies that data is transferred at irregular intervals. This means that data can be sent from one computer to another at any time (assuming they are connected). A problem arises here however.

One computer can quite easily send data at any point in time, but the receiving computer at the other end has to be ready to accept the data. To prepare the receiving computer for the incoming data, a warning signal is sent to "wake it up". This is called a start bit. Thereafter follow the actual information bearing data bits. Finally a stop bit is sent to inform the receiver that the data information has ended.

0 : 01000101 : 1

start bit   info   stop bit

All this happens automatically, but the communication programs being run by the two computers must be set up in the same way, i.e. set for the same number of data bits and stop bits.

Parity

Another concept is that of parity. Parity is used to check that a data transfer has been completed correctly. Your communications program will allow you to set up even, odd or no parity. A parity bit is added to each byte sent as a sort of control bit. An example will best explain these terms:

Character	S	a	m	
Code	1	1	1	
	0	1	1	
	1	0	0	
	0	0	1	
	0	0	1	
	1	0	0	
	1	1	1	
Parity bit	0	1	1	*For even parity*
Parity bit	1	0	0	*For odd parity*

The letter S comprises four "1"s in total. For even parity a 1 is added if necessary to make the number of 1s an even amount. Otherwise a 0 is added. So for even parity a 0 is added in this case. For odd parity however a 1 would be added to make the total number of 1s up to an odd number.

In the case of no parity nothing is added.

The parity bit is sent along with the data to the receiving computer. The receiving computer will then calculate its own parity bit and compare it with that which has been sent. If the two are alike then all is well. If not then some problem has arisen.

Once again the programs which the computers are running must be set up in the same way, i.e. both even parity, both odd parity or both no parity.

Transmission speed

The rate of transmission between two computers must be decided before the transmission takes place. It is measured in bits per second (bps) or baud. One baud is roughly the same as 1 bps. Normal transmission speeds are:

300 bps	**4800**
600	**9600**
1200	**19200**
2400	**38400**

☺ The higher the bps the quicker the data transfer and the lower the telephone costs.

300 bps is not very quick. To send or receive a 90 kbyte file would take about an hour. The same file would take around 10-15 mins at 1200 bps or only a few minutes at 9600 bps.

The highest speed you can use is determined by your modem and that of the connected computer. You can't send at 2400 bps if the receiving modem can only manage 1200 bps.

Simplex and duplex

A telephone line can be used in three different ways:- simplex, half duplex or full duplex.

Simplex means that data transfer can only be done in one direction, Videotext services that send stock market quotes over yrou TV set are an example of this.

Half duplex means that data can be sent both ways, but only in one direction at a time.

Full duplex means that data can be sent both ways and in both directions at the same time, just like when you talk on the phone.

Null-modems

It is also possible to connect two computers without using a modem. You will still need to run a communications program on both computers. You will also need to connect the two computers with a special null-modem or straight through serial cable instead of the usual modem cable.

Virus - Am I at risk?

A data virus is an *electronic disease* that can be deliberately introduced into your computer. Basically it is a small program that will destroy information on your hard disk (often at a date) or display unwanted messages on your screen.

As long as you work with your own computer and don't communicate with others you're not likely to be hit by one of these things. However, as soon as you start communicating with bulletin board system (BBS) there is a small chance that your computer may pick up a data virus that is transmitted along with another file you receive. However, the system operators usually know about most viruses and keep their bulletin boards "clean", thus minimising the risks.

Data viruses can also be passed on via a floppy disk! For example a friend might have received a program and unknowingly a virus as well, and then if he makes a copy for you on diskette the virus can be introduced into your system as well.

A user will not generally know when his/her computer has picked up a virus until something drastic happens, like the hard disk getting re-formatted.

Anti-virus programs are available. They will help you to check if any virus has been introduced.

Check-list

For successful data communications you need:

- A computer with a serial port.

- A modem attached to the serial port.

- A telephone line.

- A communications program.

- The right settings for the communications program, i.e. transmission speed, parity, number of data bits and stop bits, etc. Check your communications program's handbook for further details.

What is Windows?

In plain English, Windows lets you control and interact with your computer by pointing at symbols (called *icons*) and selecting from menus rather than having to remember the assorted DOS commands. Technically speaking, it is called a *Graphical User Interface* or GUI.

Windows also enables you to have several different programs running at the same time by starting different programs in different windows. This can be a great advantage if you often need to refer to the files in one program (a database or spreadsheet, for instance) while using another program, since you do not have to exit each program every time you swap.

There are also a number of useful accessories provided in your Windows package, including a clock, calculator, diary, drawing program and word-processor.

Windows is not a program in the normal sense of the word, like a word processor or a spreadsheet. It is a complete system, or shell, rather like DOS itself, that allows you to manage disks, documents, programs, etc. in its own way - the way that you will learn by following this course.

The advantages of Windows

The two main advantages of Windows are:

☺ Programs that are written especially for Windows have many common features. Once you have learned to operate Windows itself, or a Windows program, you will have learned how to operate all programs written for Windows.

☺ A few individuals will find it most useful to be able to run several programs at one time and be able to extract information (text or a picture) from one program and insert it into another one.

The main disadvantage is:

☺ By its very nature, Windows needs a fast computer with lots of memory if you are to be able to work quickly and effectively. You may be presented with the Insufficient memory message, i.e. the computer needs more resources. A 25 MHz 386SX computer with at least 2 Mb RAM is the minimum specification, but 4 Mb RAM is preferable, unless you are prepared to accept a slow down at times.

The Windows screen

Below is a picture of a typical Windows screen, with the individual parts labelled. Don't try to learn all these names now, you will pick them up quickly enough when you are using them. Refer back to this picture as and when you need to.

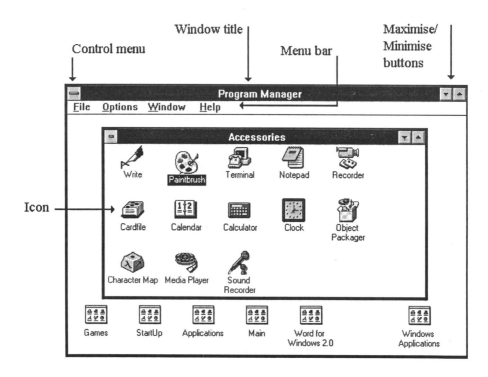

Icons and the mouse pointer

An icon is a picture that represents some kind of object - it might be a program or group of programs - that you want to use or alter in some way.

The mouse pointer is moved by the mouse, and is used to select an item that you want, whether it is a menu, an icon, a file, a window, etc. When the computer is busy, for example writing a file to disk, the pointer will change to an hourglass ($\mathbb{Z}$).

Operating Windows functions

In principle, there are two basic methods of working with Windows functions - using a mouse or using the keyboard.

You will probably find that a combination of mouse and keyboard provide the most efficient way of using Windows. It is possible to get by using just the keyboard or just the mouse, but you may find this a little slow or tedious. In this course you will learn to use both the mouse and keyboard as appropriate for the various commands.

Using the mouse

Using the mouse is clearly the easiest way to use Windows in general. You can quickly move the cursor around, open windows, open menus and make selections. There are four essential mouse operations; point, click, double-click and drag.

Operation	*Description*
Point	To point using the mouse, simply move your mouse across your desk or mouse mat (or roll your trackball). The pointer on the screen will follow your movement. To point to a particular item, a menu or icon for instance, move your mouse so that the pointer is over the desired object.
Click	To click means that you should press the LEFT mouse button ONCE. As a rule, Windows always uses the left mouse button, although some of the programs you may run under Windows will use both.
Doubleclick	Press the left mouse button TWICE in quick succession. If you do this too slowly, your computer will interpret this as two single clicks. It is possible to set how quickly you need to doubleclick using the Control Panel. This is explained later in the course.
Drag	First position the pointer over an object, press the left mouse button down and hold it down while you move the mouse. The object will be dragged around until you release the mouse button.

These four simple actions, coupled with the occasional use of the keyboard, will allow you to control Windows.

It is possible to set up the mouse for left-handed people so that the left and right-hand button functions are swapped. This course makes no allowance for such a change, so if you change the mouse you will also have to think about clicking the right-hand button instead of the left-hand button, and vice versa.

Using the keyboard

All of Windows features can be accessed using the keyboard. Instead of pointing and clicking on menus and selection boxes, for example, you can select features by pressing the right keys. To open the **File** menu, for example, you would press **Alt+F**.

Short cut keys

Some of the most important features have what is known as short cut keys. For example, if you have several windows open at the same time, you could press **Alt+Tab** to swap between the Windows. Some of these short cut keys are very useful, as you will find out.

Starting Windows

- Switch on your computer and printer.

If your computer has a menu system installed, with Windows as one of the menu options, start Windows by selecting that option in the normal way.

Otherwise, when the system prompt (C:>) appears, proceed as follows:

- Type:

  win

- Press the **Enter** key.

 It is possible to set up your computer so that it automatically starts Windows each time you start your computer. To do this, you need to adjust the file called AUTOEXEC.BAT to include the command **win** *at the end. It may be advisable to seek the help of an experienced user to do this.*

Windows will display a start up screen for a few seconds.

Program Manager

Whenever you start Windows it will always automatically start the program called **Program Manager**. This program gives you overall control of the Windows system, and it is from here that you can start to work with other applications.

☞ *It is important to note that the picture above and subsequent pictures, may differ slightly to those displayed on your screen. Do not worry about this!*

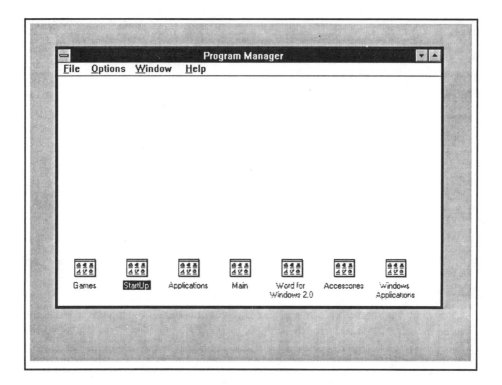

As you can see, the Program Manager window contains a number of icons. There will definitely be icons called **Main, StartUp, Accessories** and **Games**. Depending on how you installed Windows, there may also be icons called **Windows Applications** and **Non-Windows Applications**.

These icons represent groups of programs. A *Group* is essentially an electronic folder where items can be stored together for your convenience.

Restoring or expanding an icon

The simplest way of expanding an icon up to a normal window size (whether the icon represents a group or a program) is to doubleclick the icon.

● Doubleclick the **Games** icon.

☞ *If your doubleclick does not work - it may be a bit slow, or perhaps the mouse moved between the clicks -just try again. If a menu is opened, you can click on the* **Restore** *option in the menu).*

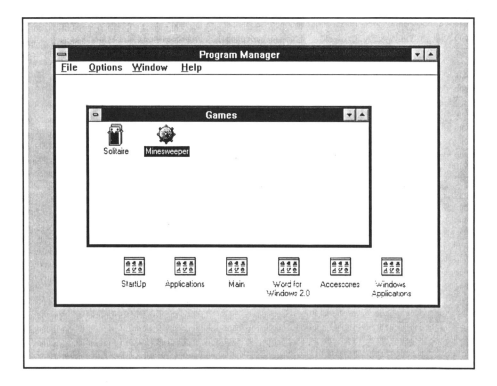

The icon expands to display a window, and you can now see the contents. There are two icons called **Solitaire** and Minesweeper, which represent two games that are supplied with your Windows package.

Minimizing a window

To shrink a window back down to an icon, you simply need to click the
Minimize button in the top right corner of the window.

☞ *When more than one window is open, each window will have its
own Minimize button, so you should make sure you click the
Minimize button for the window you wish to shrink.*

- Click the **Minimize** button on the Games window.

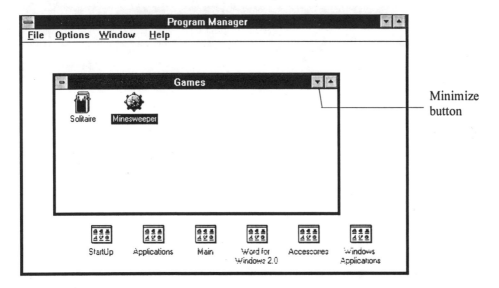

Minimize
button

The Games window returns to an icon again.

Remember

Remember the important things so far:

⊕ To expand an icon up to a group window, doubleclick the desired
icon.

⊕ To shrink a group window back down to an icon, click the window's **Minimize** button.

Starting a program

You will now start one of the programs in the Accessories window. First
of all, expand the Accessories window:

• Doubleclick the **Accessories** icon.

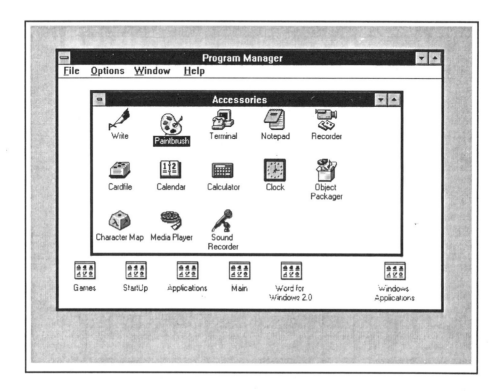

As you can see, the Accessories group contains a collection of programs
supplied with your package. This includes Write (a word-processor),
Paintbrush, Calendar, Calculator and several other programs. The easiest
way to start a program that is represented as an icon is to doubleclick the
icon. Just as doubleclicking a group icon opens the group window, so
doubleclicking a program icon opens the program.

• Doubleclick the **Write** icon.

A new window is opened for the Write program (see picture on next page).
In the normal course of events you would now start typing in a document
or would load an existing document, but for now we'll just learn how to
exit a program.

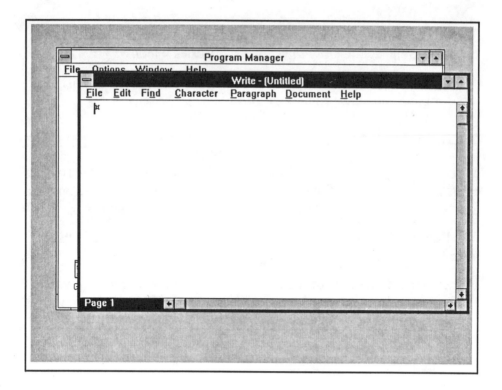

Exiting a program

To exit a program, you can either doubleclick the Control menu in the top left corner of the window, or open the **File** menu and click **Exit**.

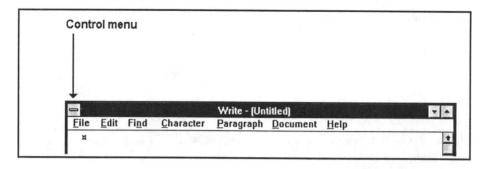

- Doubleclick the Control menu in the Write window (or open the **File** menu and click **Exit**).

The Write window will be closed, and the windows that were behind it will become visible again. Now close the Accessories window.

- Doubleclick the Control menu of the Accessories window (not the Program Manager window).

Menus

Working with Windows and Windows application programs involves the ¹constant use of menus. You will use menus to start programs, select options, activate features and commands, etc. Happily, they are very easy to use!

The Program Manager Menu bar has four menu headings. **File**, **Options**, **Window** and **Help**.

Remember that the idea of the instructions that follow is to help you get familiar with using menus, not to understand what all the options mean!

Opening Menus

There are two ways you can open a menu:

- ☺ Click on the desired menu heading.

- ☺ Hold down the **Alt** key, and press the letter that is underlined in the desired menu heading.

Do not worry if you open the wrong menu by mistake. You can either click on the correct one instead, or use the cursor control keys, **ArrowRight** and **ArrowLeft**, to move between menus.

Now open the **File** menu as follows:

- Click the **File** menu heading (or press **Alt+F**).

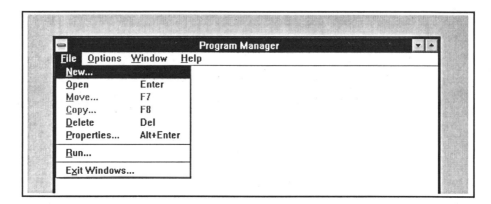

The menu is opened giving you a list of options available, in this case the options relate to files or the icons that represent them.

- Now click the **Options** menu heading (or press the **ArrowRight** key).

The next menu is opened giving a list of options that determine how the group windows will be handled.

- Click the **Window** menu heading (or press the **ArrowRight** key).

You can use the options available in the **Window** menu to control how windows will be arranged on your screen. This time, there will also be a list of the groups currently on your system.

- Click the **Help** menu heading.

You can use this menu to obtain help on the program you are working with. The information will be displayed on your screen. Using Help is described in *Appendix C*.

Closing menus

To close a menu, simply click anywhere other than on a menu (but be careful you don't activate something else by mistake), or press **Esc** twice.

- Press **Esc** twice.

Control menu

Another special menu that is not shown in the menu bar is the Control menu. All the windows in Windows have a Control menu, which you open by clicking the minus sign in the top left corner of the window.

Open the Main group as follows:

- Doubleclick the **Main** group icon.

☞ *There are now TWO different Control menus - the Control menu for the current application, i.e. Program Manager, and the Control menu for the current window, i.e. the Main group window.*

- Click the Control menu on the Main window.

The Control menu contains commands that give you control over the window - e.g. the position and size.

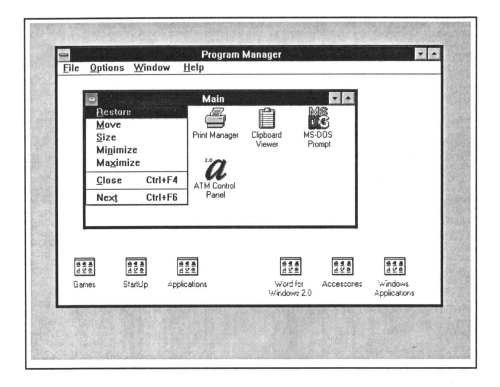

☞ *Some of the menu options may be lighter in colour, which means that they cannot be selected at the moment.*

☞ *For some menu options, you will have noticed that on the right-hand side of the menu there are some key combinations, e.g. Ctrl+F4 opposite Close. These are short cuts which you can use to give commands from the keyboard without having to open the menu.*

- Click on **Close** in the menu to close the window.

- Click the Program Manager window Control menu.

There is only one difference between this menu and the previous one - this time the short-cut to close the window is **Alt+F4**. This lets you distinguish between closing the group window you are working in as opposed to closing the Windows program itself.

- Close the menu by pressing **Esc**.

Selecting an option in a menu

Once you have a menu open, you can either click the desired option, or press the letter that is underlined in the option.

Open the Accessories and Games group windows as follows:

- Doubleclick the **Accessories** icon.

- Doubleclick the **Games** icon.

Close the Games window as follows:

- Open the Games window Control menu (not the Program Manager Control menu!) by clicking it.

- Point at the **Close** option and click.

The window should be closed. When you close a group window, it shrinks back to an icon in the Program Manager window.

- Open the Accessories window Control menu by clicking it.

- Point at the **Close** option and click.

List boxes

Many of the options in Windows menus include a list box, a drop down list from which you can select an item. You will take a look at one now, without using it.

- Doubleclick the **Main** group icon.

- Click the **File** menu - that is **File** in the menu bar, not the icon File Manager that appears in the Main group window.

- Click **Copy** in the menu that is opened.

The following is displayed on your screen:

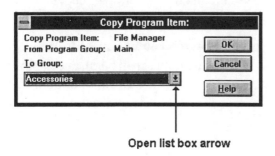

Open list box arrow

To the right of the box containing the word <u>Accessories</u> is a downward pointing arrow that opens the list box. You can scroll through the options in the list box using the up/down arrow keys, or open the list by clicking the open list box arrow.

- Click the **Open list box arrow**.

The list box will open to reveal the options.

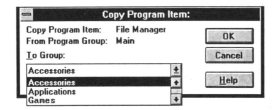

- Click one of the alternatives in the list.

This new value has become the copy destination.

- Press **Esc** or click **Cancel**, to abort the Copy command.

Dialog Boxes

Whenever Windows needs some information from you - for example it may need to know which document you want to open, confirmation of a deletion or whether you want to save a file before exiting - it will open a dialog box.

You will be given detailed instructions on how to use each dialog box at the relevant time, but here is a brief introduction to their general features:

- Open the **Control Panel** by doubleclicking its icon.

- Doubleclick the **Printers** icon.

The Printers dialog box is displayed on your screen (see picture on next page). Note that the actual names in the list of printers will depend on the ones you have installed.

This dialog box contains most of the features you will meet in Windows dialog boxes. These include lists (with or without scroll bars), check boxes, and command buttons. You can point at any of these with your mouse.

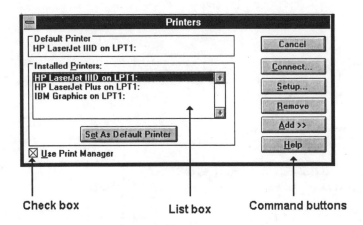

Check box   List box   Command buttons

Check boxes

Check boxes are recognisable by a square box, which may or may not contain a cross, or *check*. They are on/off switches to select a particular option. You can set the switch by clicking on the box.

- Click on the **Use Print Manager** check box.

Note that the check is removed, or added if there was not one before.

☺ If the box IS checked, the option is SELECTED.

☺ If the box IS NOT checked, the option is NOT SELECTED.

- Click on the **Use Print Manager** check box again.

Note that the check is restored, or removed again.

Check boxes are used for options that may be selected if so desired. Sometimes you will have more than one check box and you can select any number of these options, or none at all.

☞ *Note on using the keyboard:*
Pressing the **Spacebar** *will act as a click on the selected check box.*
Pressing **Tab** *will select the various buttons and boxes in order.*

Lists

Lists are used where you need to indicate which item you are working with. It is most often a list of files, but on your screen now there is a list of one or more printers. Note that one of the printers in the list will be highlighted.

Selection boxes

Selection boxes are used where you *must* select one out of several options. They are recognisable by the group of circles, one of which will contain a black dot. Clicking on an option will switch to that option.

- Click the **SetUp** button.

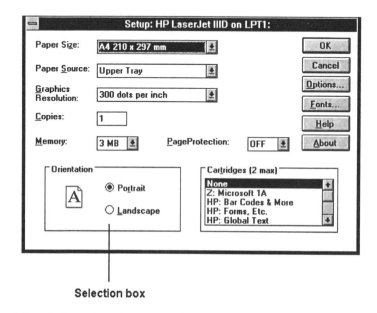

Selection box

The Orientation box contains two such selections - **Portrait** and **Landscape**. The page, of course, must be one of these, but cannot be both or none.

- Click the **Landscape** option circle to select it.

- Click the **Portrait** option circle to select it.

- Click **Cancel** to return to the previous window without saving any changes.

Command Buttons

Every dialog box has an **OK** or **Yes** button, which you can click to complete the settings or alterations you have made. Most boxes also have a **Cancel** button, which enables you to abandon the changes you have made. The current dialog box has some extra buttons - clicking these will open further dialogs.

The **Esc** key also works as a **Cancel** or **Close** button.

• Click the **Close** button.

The Printers dialog box is closed, and any alterations you made are lost.

Finally, close the Control Panel window and Main group window.

• Doubleclick the Control menu of the Control Panel window.

• Doubleclick the Control menu of the Main group window.

Note about the Save Settings on Exit option

It is possible to exit Windows with one or more windows open or just the Program Manager window as you have done so far. If the **Save Settings on Exit** option in the **Options** menu is selected, Windows records which group windows are open when you exit, and next time you start Windows it will open these windows for you. Quite simply, it remembers the state it was in on closing.

If you turn this option off, Windows will always start up as it did the last time the changes were saved. So, if you find a set-up you do like (e.g. always having the Paintbrush Accessories window open), exit Windows with the **Save Settings on Exit** option selected, to record the set-up. Then open Windows and turn the **Save Settings on Exit** option off.

See picture on next page!

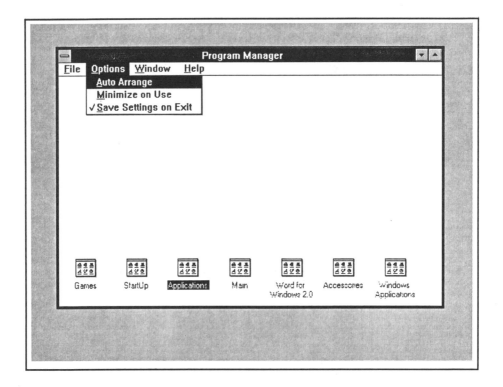

Don't worry about this setting just now.

⊕ To toggle the setting on and off, just click on the **Save Settings on Exit** option - the tick, or *check mark*, means it is selected, no check mark means it is not selected.

Exiting Windows

Exiting Windows is equivalent to exiting Program Manager. Once again, the simplest method is to doubleclick the Control menu.

• Doubleclick the Control menu of the Program Manager window.

You are now asked to confirm that you wish to exit Windows.

• Click **OK**.

Some Useful DOS Commands

This appendix summarises some of the most useful DOS commands not already described in this course. Remember that internal commands are readily available from your computer's memory, while external commands require the actual DOS program. This means that if you do not have a hard disk, for external commands you will have to insert your DOS disk in drive A to be able to use the command. External commands are marked with a * in the following table.

It is important to note that this appendix only provides a summary of each command. Many commands have other "switches" and uses. Consult your DOS manual for more information on the commands.

The following commands are described in this appendix:

*ASSIGN	Temporarily change the drive name
*BACKUP	Make back-up copy of hard disk content
*CHKDSK	Check disk
CLS	Clear screen
DATE	Change the computer's date
*DISKCOMP	Compare disks
*DISKCOPY	Copy disk
*GRAPHICS	Prepare DOS for graphics printouts
*FC	Compares files
*KEYB	Keyboard program
*KEYBUK	Keyboard program
*MODE	Communications/printer port command
*MORE	Displays one screen at a time
PATH	Gives DOS a list of drives/directories to search
*PRINT	Printing files with DOS
PROMPT	Change prompt
*RESTORE	Restore (re-copy) files to hard disk
TIME	Change the computer's time
TYPE	Type the contents of a file
*XCOPY	Copies files and subdirectories

☞ *The examples given in this appendix are just that - examples - and nothing more. You may well have to adapt the commands to suit your own needs.*

ASSIGN - Temporarily rename a drive

The ASSIGN command allows you to temporarily rename a drive. Try this if your computer has two diskette drives:

- Type:

  assign a=b

- Press the **Enter** key.

- Put any diskette with some files on in drive B.

- Type:

  dir a:

- Press the **Enter** key.

You will notice that the directory of the diskette in drive B is listed despite the fact that you gave the command **dir a:**. In other words the **assign a=b** command has instructed DOS to treat drive B as if it were drive A.

To restore the situation so that A is A and B is B do as follows:

- Type:

  assign

- Press the **Enter** key.

If you turn off your computer, then the next time you start it the drives will also behave normally, ASSIGN is only a temporary command.

ASSIGN does not work with the FORMAT and DISKCOPY commands.

BACKUP - Make a back-up copy of a hard disk

This command can be used to make back-up copies of all or some of the files on your hard disk. You can copy files that would not normally fit onto a single disk as big files are divided automatically onto a number of disks.

One disadvantage of this command is that the files on the disks cannot be used in the normal way. Instead, they must first be restored (re-copied) back into the same subdirectory on the hard disk using the RESTORE command.

Before you start, you must have a number of formatted disks available. The number you will need depends on how much you wish to copy. You should number the disks starting with 1, and they must be in the proper sequence when you restore the files to the hard disk.

- Insert the first formatted disk in drive A and type, for example:

back-up c:*.* a:	Copies all files in the current directory of C drive to drive A.
back-up c:*.* a:/s	Copies all files in the current directory of C drive all files in its subdirectories to drive A.
back-up c:*.* a:/m	Searches through all of the files in the current directory of C drive, but only copies onto drive A those files that have been changed since the last back-up copying operation.
back-up c:*.dat a:	Copies all files ending .DAT in the current directory of C drive to drive A.
back-up c:\word*. dat a:	Copies all files ending .DAT in the directory C:\WORD directory to drive A.

☞ *When you restore (re-copy) the back-up files, they must be restored to the same subdirectory from which they were copied.*

As each disk fills up, you will be prompted to insert the next disk. When the system prompt appears again, copying is finished.

CHKDSK - Check disk

When you wish to scan a disk for errors or see how much memory is available on it, you can use the CHKDSK command as follows:

- Type, for example:

  chkdsk

or

  chkdsk a:

- Press the **Enter** key.

The following is an example of what may be shown on the screen:

```
Volume xx created Feb 10, 1991 07.20a

   362496 bytes total disk space
        0 bytes in 1 hidden files
   318464 bytes in 40 user files
    44032 bytes available on disk

   655360 bytes total memory
   491136 bytes free
```

CHKDSK can also be used to correct any errors found on a disk - these will be reported if any are found when using the CHKDSK command as indicated above.

- To repair any errors type instead:

  chkdsk /f

- Press the **Enter** key.

Any lost chains (i.e. fragments of files that have got lost) can be saved as separate files which you can then use.

CLS - Clear screen

This command clears the screen.

- Type:

  cls

- Press the **Enter** key.

DATE - Change the computer's date

The computer keeps a record of the date. You can change the computer's date as follows:

- Type:

  date

- Press the **Enter** key.

```
Current date is Thu 23-05-1993
Enter new date (dd-mm-yy):_
```

☞ *The date format may be different on your computer, e.g. yy-mm-dd or mm-dd-yy, depending on which country it is set up for.*

You have two choices. Either you confirm the displayed date, or you enter an alternative date, i.e. the right one. Some programs depend on the computer's date being correct, and this date will also be used when files are saved to record the creation or change date in the disk's directory.

To confirm the displayed date, do the following:

- Press the **Enter** key.

To enter a different date, do the following:

- Type in the desired date, putting hyphens between the day, month and year. For example:

  27-05-93

- Press the **Enter** key.

DISKCOMP - Compare disks

You can compare the contents of two disks after you have copied them, useful if you have run DISKCOPY (see below) and wish to check that all went well.

☞ *Both disks need to be the same type to use DISKCOMP.*

- Type:

  diskcomp a: b:

- Press the **Enter** key.

The following will appear on the screen:

```
Insert first disk in drive A:   Insert second disk in drive B:

Strike any key when ready
```

- Insert the first disk in drive A.

- Insert the disk that is to be compared with the first disk in drive B.

- Press the **Enter** key.

When the following appears on the screen, the comparison has shown that the contents of the disks are identical.

```
Disk compare OK

Compare more disks (Y/N)?
```

- Press the **N** key if you wish to conclude comparison.

- Press the **Y** key if you wish to compare other disks.

DISKCOPY - Copy disk

You can copy the entire contents of a disk onto another disk by means of DISKCOPY. The disk onto which you are copying need not be formatted, since this is done automatically by DISKCOPY.

☞ *Both disks have to be the same type to use DISKCOPY.*

- Type:

  diskcopy a: b:

- Press the **Enter** key.

The following will appear on your screen:

```
Insert source disk in drive A:
Insert target disk in drive B:

Strike any key when ready _
```

- Insert the disk containing what you wish to copy into disk drive A.

- Insert the disk onto which you wish to copy into disk drive B.

- Press the **Enter** key.

When the following appears on your screen, copying has been completed:

```
Copy another (Y/N)?_
```

- Press the **N** key if you wish to conclude copying. Press the **Y** key if you wish to copy another disk.

FC - Compare files

Compares two files or two groups of files and displays any differences. FC can be particularly useful for combating computer viruses.

To compare two files, one in the current subdirectory of the hard disk and one on a diskette in drive B, proceed as follows:

• Type, for example:

  fc myfile.txt b:myfile.txt

Note that the two files do not necessarily have to have the same name.

GRAPHICS - Prepares DOS for graphics printouts

GRAPHICS lets you print a graphics display on your printer using the Print Screen key.

The following applies for a IBM Proprinter/Graphics printer.

• Type:

  graphics

This activates the graphics command, but it does take up some memory. To print a graphics display then do as follows:

• Press the **Print Screen** key.

Note: The GRAPHICS command can be put in your AUTOEXEC.BAT file.

KEYB - Keyboard program

Loads a keyboard program for a specific country, for example:

keyb us	U.S. (default)
keyb uk	U.K.
keyb fr	France
keyb it	Italy
keyb sp	Spain
keyb po	Portugal
keyb sg	Swiss-German
keyb sf	Swiss-French
keyb dk	Denmark
keyb no	Norway
keyb sw	Sweden

The **keyb** command, for the keyboard you normally use, should be put in your AUTOEXEC.BAT file. You can also change the keyboard by typing the command at the DOS prompt, e.g.:

> **keyb it**

to use the Italian keyboard layout.

KEYBUK - Keyboard program for DOS versions before 3.3

For DOS versions 3.3 and later use the KEYB command as above. The KEYBUK command works as for the KEYB command with the exception that the two country specific letters are part of the actual command word rather than a parameter. If you have an earlier version than DOS 3.3, consult your DOS manual for more details.

MODE - Communications/printer port set-up

MODE is an extensive command that covers far more that is described here.

To re-direct a printout from the parallel printer port (LPT1) to the serial port (COM1) type the following command:

mode lpt1:=com1:

To set up a serial port with the following parameters;

speed (baud)	9600
parity	none
data bits	8
stop bits	1

mode com1:96,n,8,1

There are the most normal settings for serial printers and even modems.

MORE - Displays one screen at a time

MORE limits a screen output to one screen at a time - rather like the **dir/p** command. It is useful in conjunction with the TYPE command when you are displaying longer files. The display halts at each full screen and waits until you press any key before continuing.

The following example will display the file MY.TXT one screen at a time:

type my.txt | more

Note that the normal TYPE command is separated from the MORE command with a bar character (|).

PATH - Gives DOS a search path

PATH can be used to give DOS a list of directories and drives to search when trying to start a program or batch file. Here is an example:

path c:\;c:\batch;c:\dos;c:\word

When starting a program or batch file DOS will automatically first look in the current drive/subdirectory. If it does not find the file it will then run through the list provided in the PATH command in the order started.

The PATH command is normally added to your AUTOEXEC.BAT file.

PRINT - Uses DOS to print files

Prints files via DOS to a printer (not PostScript printers). To print the file MYFILE.TXT give the following command:

print myfile.txt

To re-direct the printout to a specific printer port type, for example;

print myfile.txt /d:com1

or

print myfile.txt /d:lpt2

PROMPT - Change prompt

You can change the system prompt from the familiar A> or C> if so desired. If you are using a hard disk, there are many advantages to having the system prompt indicate which subdirectory you are in.

• Check that the system prompt appears on the screen.

• Type:

prompt pg

This changes the system prompt so that it presents the current subdirectory.

For example: C:\WORD

• Press the **Enter** key.

```
C:>\WORD _
```

It is advisable to insert this command in your AUTOEXEC.BAT so that this type of explicit system prompt will always come up when you start your computer. There are a number of different ways to arrange the system prompt, and they are explained in the DOS manual that came with your computer.

A favourite with a lot of computer hackers is:

prompt $t pg

This changes the system prompt so that it presents both the current subdirectory and the correct time according to your computer's system clock! It's great if you're one of those persons who ends up missing appointments or a normal night's sleep due to spending too much time working on your computer. If you want to be reminded of the date instead of the time, just substitute a "d" for the "t" in the above command.

To intimidate your friends who are afraid of computers, try:

prompt WHAT IS YOUR WISH MASTER? pg

By now you should be able to guess what this will do.

RESTORE - Restore back-up files to hard disk

RESTORE is a DOS command that is usually kept on a hard disk (otherwise, it is on the DOS disk). It is used to restore (re-copy) files that have been backed up (copied) using the BACKUP command. The RESTORE command can be used for all types of files that have been backed up by means of the BACKUP command, although files that are write-protected can cause trouble.

Before you start, you must have your back-up disks ready, and you must use them in numerical sequence starting with 1. The sequence is important.

 Note:
Remember that you can only restore files to the subdirectory from which you backed them up.

• Insert the first disk in drive A.

- Type, for example:

restore a: c:*.*	This restores all files from drive A to the current directory on the hard disk.
restore a: c:*.*/s	This restores all files from drive A to the current directory on the hard disk together with all the subdirectories from which the files were originally copied.
restore a: c:*.*/p	Same as above, but /p causes the computer to *prompt* you, which means that it will ask whether each file that has been changed since you made the back-up copy should be restored to the earlier form on the back-up disk.
restore a: c:*.txt	This restores all files ending .TXT from drive A to the directory on the hard disk from which they were copied.
restore a: c:\word*.dat	This restores all files ending .DAT from drive A to the directory C:\WORD.

- Press the **Enter** key.

You are now asked to insert the first disk, and as soon as it is copied you are asked to insert the next, etc.

When the system prompt appears again, copying is completed.

TIME - Change the computer's time

The computer keeps track of the current time. You can alter the time as follows:

- Type:

  time

- Press the **Enter** key.

```
Current time is Wed 08:17:35:26
Enter correct time:_
```

You have two choices, either confirm the shown time, or enter a different time.

To confirm the displayed time, do the following:

- Press the **Enter** key.

To enter a new time, do the following:

- Type in the desired time, for example:

  19:18

Note that it is sufficient to give only the hour, and the minutes.

- Press the **Enter** key.

The major use for TIME is to be able to display the time as part of your DOS prompt. Also, the creation time of a file is always shown in the directory display.

TYPE - Type the contents of a file

The type command gives you a way of looking at the contents of a file. TYPE is an internal DOS command and is readily available. The following example assumes that you have a disk in drive A, with the file TEST1.DOC on it.

- Type the following:

  type a:test1.doc

- Press the **Enter** key.

The contents of the file will be displayed on your screen:

```
Hi there,

This is just one of those boring old example texts.

Bye.
```

To display longer files one screenful at a time use TYPE together with the MORE command as explained under the MORE heading.

XCOPY - Copies subdirectories

XCOPY copies files and complete subdirectories if they exist. The XCOPY command on its own will only copy files from the current drive/directory.

xcopy c:*.* a:

The /s switch allows non-empty subdirectories to be copied. The /e switch allows empty subdirectories to be copied and must be used together with the /s switch. Use the following command to copy all directories, including empty directories from a diskette in drive A to a diskette in drive B:

xcopy c:*.* a: /s /e

Some Common DOS Error Messages

When you're working with a computer, things do not always work out as expected: the wrong disk, a forgotten colon, a wrong filename, etc. DOS has a set of error messages to tell you when you've issued an *illegal command*. Don't worry about the command being labelled illegal, all this means is that you've made a minor error in typing it.

This appendix lists the most common error messages, and suggests what you might have done wrong. The error messages are in alphabetical order.

 The actual text of the error message may vary in some cases from that which is shown on your screen. Also, this list is by no means complete. Refer to your DOS manual for information on other messages.

Abort, Retry, Ignore, Fail?

This message is always displayed with a device error message, e.g. a printer or disk drive message. If you know what caused the problem, e.g. diskette upside down or write-protected, then take the necessary action before continuing as follows:

A Aborts the current operation and may even stop the program altogether and return you to the DOS prompt.

R Retry the operation. Select this option if you think you have cured the problem, or suspect the problem was temporary.

I Ignore the operation and pretend that the problem never arose. This will allow the program to continue but may cause many unexpected problems thereafter. It is recommended to try the Fail option rather than this.

F This option was added to DOS 3.3 versions and later. It continues with the program but does inform DOS of the apparent failure.

Attempted write-protection violation

The disk you tried to format was write- protected. Change disks or disable the protection by removing the write-protect label from a 5.25" disk or moving the slide position from a 3.5" disk.

Bad command or file name

You have typed in a program name or command that doesn't exist in the specified, or current, directory or drive. The computer cannot find what you have typed. Check your spelling.

You may also be able to rectify the problem by extending the PATH command in your AUTOEXEC.BAT file especially if the computer is not finding a certain program or batch file - see chapter on batch files for further explanation of PATH.

Bad or missing command interpreter

The file COMMAND.COM cannot be found on the disk that DOS is being started with. You will need to copy this file to the relevant diskette, which for diskette based systems may even involve creating a new system diskette from scratch using your original DOS diskette.

Cannot load COMMAND.COM, system halted

DOS tried to re-load the file COMMAND.COM but could not do so. Reboot the computer and if the message persists then use a system diskette and copy this file to the relevant disk, which for diskette based systems may even involve creating a new system diskette from scratch using your original DOS diskette.

Compare error on disk

DOS has found a difference between two disks you were comparing with the DISKCOMP command.

Data error reading drive X

The computer cannot read information from the stated disk. Try typing R to retry a few times. If that doesn't work, then type A for abort.

Divide overflow

> A program tried to divide by zero or there was an internal logical problem inside the computer. Sometimes this may be caused by a "glitch" (temporary hiccough) in RAM and re-booting the computer will solve the problem although you will loose any unsaved work.

Drive not ready error

> Normally for diskette drives - DOS is reporting that the drive is not ready for use. The drive may not be properly closed or the diskette may be badly positioned.

Duplicate filename

> You tried to rename a file but have given it the same name as another existing file, or the specified file cannot be found. Check the file names on the disk, and try again.

Error in EXE file

> The program file is damaged. The only thing to do is to re-copy or re-install the program.

File cannot be copied onto itself

> When trying to copy a file you gave the target file (copy) the same name as the source file. Give the copy a different name.

File creation error

> You tried to write a file but: the directory was full, the disk was full, the original file was a read only file and thus could not be overwritten or the disk is physically damaged. Try removing some other unwanted files to create free space. If a read only file exists with the same filename you cannot write over this file - try giving the file a different filename.

File not found

> The computer cannot find the file that you specified. Check that you have entered the filename correctly.

Format failure

> The disk cannot be formatted correctly. It's probably defective.

General failure error

> Something went wrong but DOS doesn't know what! For diskettes check to see that the drive and diskette types are compatible and that the disk is inserted correctly and the latch closed. Is the diskette properly formatted?

Illegal device name

> You have specified a device name that does not currently exist in your computer system. Check your typing.

Incorrect number of parameters

> You specified too many or too few options in the command.

Insufficient disk space

> The specified disk is full. Erase some files from the disk or try another one. If you get this command frequently on your hard disk, it's time to consider buying a second hard disk or upgrading to a larger one.

Insufficient memory

> There is not enough memory in your computer to perform the specified operation. This either means that you need more memory (today there's no excuse for having less than 640 kb) or that you're using some memory resident software that has to be unloaded before the particular program you're now trying to use can run.

Invalid date

> You specified an invalid date in response to the DATE command.

Invalid directory

> The directory you specified does not exist. Type it again more carefully.

Invalid drive specification

> The drive you specified doesn't exist.

Invalid path

> The pathname you specified does not exist.

Invalid number of parameters

> You specified too many or too few options in the command.

Invalid parameters

>One or more of the command parameters is wrong.

Invalid path

>The pathname you specified does not exist.

Invalid time

>You specified an invalid time in response to the TIME command.

Non-system disk or disk error. Replace and strike any key when ready

>You tried to start your computer with a non-system disk in drive A. Take the disk out and try again.

No paper error writing device

>Your printer is out of paper, is not switched on, or is not in the PRINT READY status.

Read fault error reading drive X

>The computer is unable to read data from the specified drive. This could be a temporary read error caused by your computer. Hit R for retry.

>If this happens again, you've somehow damaged your disk and you probably won't be able to recover the data on it unless you can get help with a friend who is very knowledgeable and has the right software. Therefore, go to your back-up disk. What? You don't have a back-up disk? We warned you this would happen!

☝ *If this happens when you're trying to read a disk that wasn't created in your computer, the problem may be that either your disk drive or the disk drive in the other computer is out of alignment. Try reading the disks on the machine on which it was created and/or on other machines. If it can be read on these but not on yours, have a technician check your drive's alignment.*

Target disk is unusable

>The disk you tried to format is defective.

Target disk is write-protected

>The computer tried to write information on a disk that is write-protected.

Unable to create directory

> The computer cannot create the specified directory. It may already exist, or you may have specified a name with more than 8 characters or with a space in it.

Write fault error writing drive X

> The computer was unable to write data to the specified drive. This is usually a computer error. Try R retry. If it happens again the disk may be damaged.

Write protect error writing drive X

> The computer tried to write information on a disk that is write-protected.

Batch Files

You may well have heard the term *batch file* and wondered what it really meant, or even have some understanding but assumed it was too difficult to get involved in. In this chapter the simplicity and usefulness of batch files is revealed. You can learn how quickly you can create batch files and by studying a few examples you will soon be able to write your own.

The all-important batch file called AUTOEXEC.BAT has been looked at in the chapter **System Disks and Files**. Although its contents are very important, it is just a batch file like any other.

Finally, the last section of this chapter delves deeper into the world of batch files and presents the batch file commands that are available if you wish to start creating small batch file programs.

What is a batch file

A batch file is a sort of auto-pilot that can perform several DOS commands in sequence. If you are regularly typing in a series of DOS commands, for example to change directories and start a certain program, then you should think about creating a batch file to do the repetitive work for you. Then, instead of typing in the commands, you only need to type the name of your batch file and the rest is done for you.

Here is a quick example: Assume that you have a computer game on your hard disk called CHASE.EXE, and that it is stored in a subdirectory called \GAMES\CHASE. To start the game, you would normally have to go through the following steps:

- Type **c:**   to make C the current drive.

- Press the **Enter** key.

- Type **cd \games\chase**   to move to the CHASE subdirectory.

- Press the **Enter** key.

- Type **chase**   to start the game.

- Press the **Enter** key.

This is not really hard work, but nevertheless can cause a few problems for a user not really conversant with DOS commands. The whole process could be replaced by one batch file named CHASE.BAT. The batch file would have the following contents:

```
c:
cd \games\chase
chase
cd\
```

Comparing the batch file to the commands above you will see that exactly the same three commands are used. A fourth command, **cd**, is added to the end - this changes the current directory back to the root directory at when you exit the CHASE program. So batch files can follow commands to start a program and even resume control when that program is ended.

The greatest difference is that when you wished to start the game you would only have to type one command, chase, and then press the **Enter** key.

Using batch files to start programs that otherwise involve giving three or four DOS commands is one obvious use. More examples will be given later on in this chapter, and examples of batch files will also appear in other chapters.

How to create batch files

There are three different ways of creating a batch file, they are:

⊕   Using your word processor.

⊕   Using the DOS command COPY.

⊕   Using the DOS programs EDLIN or EDIT.

Each of the methods is explained briefly below.

Using your word processor

Using your word processor has the advantage that you already know how to use it. It is easy to create both small and large batch files especially if your batch file contains information to be displayed on the screen and you wish to give it some sort of layout.

However, there is one restriction on using your word processor - the file you produce has to be an ASCII file. An ASCII file is quite simply a clean text file free from any special control characters. Most word processors add their own such control characters to texts and hide them automatically from you. However, most word processors also have the ability to produce ASCII code. You may need to check your word processor manual to find out about this.

You can also use an Editor program, which is a kind of word processor anyway. Editors always produce clean ASCII files.

To produce a batch file with your word processor/editor do as follows:

☺ Start your word processor and open a new file.

☺ Type in the commands.

☺ Save the file as an ASCII file giving it a suitable name with a .BAT extension, e.g. CHASE.BAT.

Note that the batch file should be saved in the root directory of your hard disk, or if you have one, in a special subdirectory called \BATCH where you gather all your batch files.

If you have a diskette based system you should put the batch file on the diskette containing the relevant program.

Using the COPY command

Normally you use the COPY command to copy files to and from diskettes and hard disks. By using the COPY command together with the word CON (short for console, i.e. your keyboard), you still copy a file, but that file comes directly from the keyboard as you type it in.

It is very quick and easy to create a file using COPY. COPY is an internal DOS command, which means that it is always readily available even if you are using a diskette based system. It is ideal for creating small batch files containing just a few lines, or larger ones if you type carefully and accurately. The reason is that the COPY command allows you to enter text one line at a time and having confirmed that line by pressing the **Enter** key, you cannot go back to it to change it in any way. If you make a mistake the only thing to do is to end the file and start all over again.

As an example of how to create a file in this way, do as follows:

- Type:

  copy con example.txt

- Press the **Enter** key.

This has opened a file called EXAMPLE.TXT, i.e. not a batch file in this case. The cursor has moved down to the next blank line is waiting for you to type in the first line.

```
C:\copy con example.txt
_
```

- Type:

  I am creating this file using the COPY command

At this point, i.e. before you confirm the line by pressing the **Enter** key, you can still edit the line by deleting with the **Backspace** key.

- Use the **Backspace** key to remove command, but not the space after COPY.

- Now type:

  CON command.

- Press the **Enter** key.

The first line is now confirmed and cannot be edited.

- Type:

  This is the second line

- Press the **Enter** key.

- Type:

  Bye for now

- Press the **Enter** key.

That is enough for this file. To end the file do as follows:

- Press the **F6** key.

Pressing the **F6** key tells DOS that you do not wish to enter any more lines. **F6** is represented on the screen by ^Z. The result of your work should look like this:

```
C:\copy con example.txt
I am creating this file using the COPY command
This is the second line
Bye for now
^Z
```

- Finally, press the **Enter** key to end the whole process.

You have now created a text file. To assure yourself of the file's existence, do as follows:

- Type:

    type example.txt

- Press the **Enter** key.

The file will be displayed on your screen.

If you wish to delete the file, do as follows:

- Type:

    del example.txt

- Press the **Enter** key.

The file will be deleted from your diskette or hard disk.

Using EDLIN and EDIT

EDLIN is a line processor supplied with DOS. It lies between a word processor and using the COPY CON command. You can enter commands line by line, as with COPY CON, but each line can be edited just as with a word processor. However, it is not as simple as moving the cursor up and down. A command has to be given to move to any specific line, and you will inevitably need to learn a small set of commands to work with EDLIN.

EDIT is a much improved and easy to use editor program.

EDLIN and EDIT are not covered in this course. If you wish to find out more about them now, you should consult your DOS manual.

How batch files work

A batch file is a special file containing a series of commands. All batch files must have a filename with a .BAT extension, i.e. CHASE.BAT, WORD.BAT, FMT.BAT, etc.

When you wish to run a batch file you simply type the name of that batch file - just the main filename is necessary, you do not need to type the .BAT extension part of the filename. For example, type chase, word, fmt, etc.

When DOS finds the batch file (assuming you have the right diskette loaded or have not hidden the batch file in a subdirectory somewhere on your hard disk), it reads the commands one line at a time and tries to execute that command. If, for any reason, DOS cannot follow the command, it will issue a message and move on to the next command on the next line.

If during the batch file process you remove the diskette containing the batch file, you may for example use the batch file to start another program that requires access to other diskettes, then you will need to re-insert the batch file diskette before DOS continues with the next command.

☺ Batch files can be aborted by pressing **Ctrl+C**.

An example batch file

Try creating some of the following example batch file using the COPY CON command. Assume you want to set up a batch file to start the CRASH.EXE program supplied on your diskette, giving the batch file the name CRASH.BAT and storing it in the root directory of your hard disk.

- Make sure the DOS prompt C:\> is shown.

- Type:

    copy con crash.bat

- Press the **Enter** key.

You will first introduce the PAUSE command, which means that DOS will stop and wait for a key to be pressed. This gives you the opportunity to display a message. The text Strike any key to continue is added automatically by DOS on the next line immediately after your message.

- Type:

  pause Insert your exercise diskette in drive A

- Press the **Enter** key.

Change to drive A.

- Type:

  a:

- Press the **Enter** key.

Now add the line that starts the program.

- Type:

  crash.exe

- Press the **Enter** key.

Next change back to drive C - this will happen when the program is exited.

- Type:

  c:

- Press the **Enter** key.

Finally, finish creating the batch file.

- Press the **F6** key.

- Press the **Enter** key.

The batch file is now complete.

Running the batch file

Try running the batch file:

- Type:

  crash

- Press the **Enter** key.

You are now asked to insert the exercise diskette and then press any key.

- Insert the disk and press a key.

The program should now start.

• Just quit the program for now.

You should be returned to the C:\> prompt.

More about batch files

This appendix was a very brief look at batch files. With the domination of Windows, batch files these days are on thier way out, but there is more information about them in your DOS manual.

Index

Free exercise diskette

There is a diskette which accompanies this book that contains the original files and programs needed to fully follow the exercises in this book.

The exercise diskette should be attached to the inside back cover.

If the diskette is missing, you can obtain one from *PC Productions Limited* as follows:

fax PC Productions on **01453-755400**

or,

write to:

PC Productions Limited
The Clock House
Stafford Mill
STROUD
GL5 2AZ

When requesting the diskette, proof of purchase will be needed. Ask for the **PCCR Survival Guide v5** diskette. Unless you say otherwise, you will be sent a 3.5" diskette.